Hell and Divine Goodness

Hell and Divine Goodness

A Philosophical-Theological Inquiry

James S. Spiegel

CASCADE *Books* • Eugene, Oregon

HELL AND DIVINE GOODNESS
A Philosophical-Theological Inquiry

Copyright © 2019 James S. Spiegel. All rights reserved. Except for brief quotations in critical publications or reviews, no part of this book may be reproduced in any manner without prior written permission from the publisher. Write: Permissions, Wipf and Stock Publishers, 199 W. 8th Ave., Suite 3, Eugene, OR 97401.

Cascade Books
An Imprint of Wipf and Stock Publishers
199 W. 8th Ave., Suite 3
Eugene, OR 97401

www.wipfandstock.com

PAPERBACK ISBN: 978-1-5326-4095-7
HARDCOVER ISBN: 978-1-5326-4096-4
EBOOK ISBN: 978-1-5326-4097-1

Cataloging-in-Publication data:

Name: Spiegel, James S., 1963-, author.

Title: Hell and divine goodness : a philosophical-theological inquiry / James S. Spiegel.

Description: Eugene, OR : Cascade Books, 2019 | Includes bibliographical references and index.

Identifiers: ISBN 978-1-5326-4095-7 (paperback) | ISBN 978-1-5326-4096-4 (hardcover) | ISBN 978-1-5326-4097-1 (ebook)

Subjects: LCSH: Hell—Christianity. | Philosophy | Hell—Biblical teaching. | Immortality. | God—Goodness.

Classification: LCC BT836.2 S695 2019 (print) | LCC BT836.2 (ebook)

Manufactured in the U.S.A.   04/02/19

This book is dedicated to
the memory of Edward W. Fudge.

Contents

Preface | ix
Acknowledgments | xi

Introduction | 1
1 Biblical Considerations | 8
2 Hell and Divine Justice | 33
3 Hell and the Problem of Evil | 57
4 Hell, Immortality, and Salvation | 80
5 Hell and Heavenly Bliss | 105
Conclusion | 124

Bibliography | 127
Index | 133

Preface

Recently, I bumped into a former student who inquired about what I was up to on the scholarly front. When I informed him that I was in the process of writing a book on hell, he winced and offered a faltering "okay" in response. As I went on to briefly explain the aims and general content of the book he listened politely, but it was apparent that he considered the topic to be odd and perhaps irrelevant to the more serious concerns of contemporary philosophy and theology. Perhaps, like some folks, he would even regard exploration of the doctrine of hell to be a waste of time, because, well, there is no such thing as hell.

The subject of this book is no doubt questionable to many people. For some, the very idea of an afterlife is problematic, whether due to their basic commitment to naturalism, a strongly empiricist epistemological orientation, or an association of the doctrine of hell with shallow fundamentalist thinking. Others find the topic dubious because, although they believe in an afterlife, they are skeptical about the idea of divine judgment. Even people who are otherwise theologically serious might balk at the notion that God would not forgive some people for the wrongs they have committed in this life.

Yet both the reality of the afterlife and the final divine judgment of the human race are clearly affirmed in Scripture. The book of Ecclesiastes concludes with the statement, "Fear God and keep his commandments, for this is the duty of all mankind. For God will bring every deed into judgment, including every hidden thing, whether it is good or evil" (Eccl 12:13–14). And the apostle Paul says, "we make it our goal to please [God], whether we are at home in the body or away from it. For we must all appear before the judgment seat of Christ, so that each of us may receive what is due us for the things done while in the body, whether good or bad" (2 Cor 5:9–10). So skepticism regarding the afterlife and divine judgment is arguably just a symptom of a deeper skepticism about the authority of Scripture. But even among those who recognize biblical authority there is much to ponder and debate concerning the afterlife and the consequences of God's final judgment of human beings: Who goes to heaven? Who goes to hell? What do these respective destinies entail? What are the divine criteria for determining who goes where? What is the nature of hell's torments? How long must the denizens of hell suffer? Is there an opportunity for escape? Such are some of the questions concerning the dark side of what is sometimes called *personal eschatology*—a subject that is as important as it is fascinating.

As a philosophical-theological inquiry into the doctrine of hell, this book aims to provide a close analysis of some key issues related to the subject, especially those that are axiological in nature—issues related to what is right, good, and just in relation to God's decisions in damnation. Accordingly, I have titled the book *Hell and Divine Goodness*.

Acknowledgments

Portions of this book appeared in some of my earlier publications. Parts of chapter 2 were drawn from my article "Annihilation, Everlasting Torment, and Divine Justice," *International Journal of Philosophy and Theology* 76 (2015) 241–48. Portions of chapter 3 were drawn from my "Hell and the Problem of Eternal Evil," *Toronto Journal of Theology* 31 (2015) 239–48. And a section in chapter 4 appeared in my essay "Making the Philosophical Case for Conditionalism" in *A Consuming Passion: Essays on Hell and Immortality in Honor of Edward Fudge* (Pickwick, 2015). My thanks to each of these publishers for granting permission to incorporate these materials into this volume.

I want to express my gratitude to Christopher Date and Richard Smith for their helpful input regarding chapter 1. Thanks as well to my former students Scott Cleveland, Luke Tatone, and Caleb Peery for their encouragement and stimulating input over the years. And thanks to my colleagues in the department of Biblical Studies, Christian Ministries, and Philosophy at Taylor University for their ongoing collegiality and personal support.

Finally, I thank my wife, Amy, my three sons, Bailey, Sam, and Andrew, and my daughter Maggie, for their love, encouragement, and good humor.

Introduction

The subject of personal eschatology is one of great practical concern for each of us. After all, this earthly life is going to end for you, me, and everyone we know. So what comes next? Philosophers and theologians have been pondering this question for all of recorded human history, and undoubtedly those outside scholarly circles have wrestled with the question for just as long. The Bible's detailed attention to issues concerning the afterlife only reinforce this interest, as we are repeatedly reminded that how we live now will have eternal ramifications. Heavenly hope for the faithful is heavily emphasized throughout the biblical corpus, as are warnings of damnation for the wicked. And devotees of all of the major Abrahamic religions—Judaism, Christianity, and Islam—generally agree that what we believe about such matters properly impacts our lives *now*.

Many popular volumes have been published in recent years regarding the happy aspect of the afterlife binary—heaven. In contrast, books dealing with hell are never very popular, usually limited to consumption by scholars in theology and philosophy of religion. This is not surprising, since the vast majority of people who believe in an afterlife expect to ultimately land in heaven rather than hell. The subject of hell is nonetheless significant for even the most devout among us for several reasons. For one thing, the truth about hell—why people go there, how long it lasts, God's purposes in creating hell, etc.—tells us a lot about the divine nature, specifically God's goodness and purposes related to the creation and redemption of human beings. Secondly, the doctrine of hell has implications for how we should think about the problem of evil and the ultimate significance of the moral life. While our motivation to live a virtuous life need not be entirely determined by our concern to avoid hell, convictions about the reality of damnation will likely have a sobering effect on the morally serious person.

Within the Christian theological tradition there has always been a variety of perspectives on hell, and these views may be variously distinguished according to such things as positions regarding the purpose of hell, the nature of hell, and the duration of hell's torments for the damned. Historically, the most controversial point of contention among Christians has pertained to how long the damned are punished. This will likewise be the main concern of this book, though we will also attend to several other questions. As for the views that Christians have held regarding the question of hell's duration, there are three standard positions. *Traditionalists* maintain that the suffering of the damned lasts forever. They have also tended to affirm the inescapability of this condition of conscious torment. In other words, on most versions of the traditional view, there is no way out of hell. In contrast, the view known as conditional immortalism, or simply *conditionalism*, says the suffering of the damned lasts for a finite period of time, after which the damned are completely annihilated (hence the view is often referred to as "annihilationism"). Like traditionalists, proponents of conditionalism usually maintain that hell is inescapable, though they deny it is permanent, terminating as it does in the irreversible destruction of the damned. Finally, there is *universalism*, the view that eventually everyone goes to heaven. Some universalists deny the reality of hell altogether, while *restorationist* universalists affirm the reality of hell and believe that people suffer there for a finite time until either they repent or are otherwise restored to right standing with God. Note that throughout this book I will only consider restorationist universalism, since non-hell versions of universalism do not appear to be biblically plausible views. Therefore, all references to universalism are references to the restorationist form of this view, unless otherwise noted.

SOME HISTORICAL CONSIDERATIONS

The doctrine of hell, though important, is properly considered a secondary theological issue. Most Christian theologians would identify such doctrines as the divine Trinity, the hypostatic union, and the resurrection of Christ to be central tenets of the faith, definitive for theological orthodoxy, as evidenced in the repeated affirmations of these doctrines in the classical creeds of the Christian church. Among secondary issues—those which are important but non-creedal—are views regarding biblical anthropology, the atonement, eschatology, and the doctrine of hell. This fact warrants our

Introduction

recognizing some latitude when it comes to personal convictions on these issues. Another reason for latitude on the doctrine of hell in particular is the fact that in the first few centuries of church history all three views were affirmed by multiple church leaders, with conditionalism enjoying the strongest advocacy of the ante-Nicene period. According to Le Roy Froom, early conditionalists included Clement of Rome, Ignatius of Antioch, Barnabas of Alexandria, Hermas of Rome, Polycarp of Smyrna, Justin Martyr, Tatian of Assyria, Theophilus of Antioch, Melito of Sardis, Polycrates of Ephesus, Irenaeus of Lyons, and Novatian of Rome.[1] During this period, there was less support for eternal conscious torment, though such notables as Athenagoras of Athens and Tertullian of Carthage endorsed the view. Universalism appears to have been as widely defended as traditionalism among influential church leaders in this period, affirmed by such thinkers as Origen of Alexandria and Pamphilus of Caesarea. The post-Nicene patristics were likewise divided over the doctrine of hell, with some of the most influential church fathers advocating universalism, e.g., Eusebius of Caesaria, Didymus of Alexandria, and Gregory of Nyssa.

But everything changed with the arrival of Augustine, whose influence on the subsequent history of Christian thought was unparalleled for the next eight centuries. Throughout the medieval and modern periods, Augustine's convictions on the doctrine of hell remained preeminent with relatively few outliers, though since the late nineteenth century there has been a growing resurgence of defenses of non-traditionalist views. I draw two important lessons from these historical facts. The first is that the traditional doctrine of hell as eternal conscious torment deserves considerable respect if only because it has been advocated by such theological giants as Augustine, Anselm, Aquinas, Luther, Calvin, and Edwards. This fact by itself might reasonably create a presumption in favor of the view. However, any such presumption should be tempered by the fact that so many early church fathers were proponents of the other two views, especially conditionalism. Aside from the strong numbers of church fathers who advocated non-traditional views, their *chronological proximity* to the apostles also contributes to the epistemic force of divided patristic opinions on the doctrine of hell.

Of course, even if there is a general historical consensus favoring a particular view of hell, this does not settle the matter. As a theological issue, scriptural evidence is of the first importance, and it is always possible that

1. See Froom, *Conditionalist Faith*.

a fresh consideration of biblical arguments might reveal dimensions of the issue that have not been sufficiently appreciated by proponents of the historically dominant view. As an issue that is also deeply philosophical, there might be moral, metaphysical, or epistemic aspects of the issue of hell that have been previously overlooked. Hence the need for another study of the subject, and I hope to highlight some significant philosophical problems with the traditional view of hell and, to a lesser extent, the universalist view.

THESIS AND BOOK SUMMARY

Before summarizing my thesis and argumentative strategy, let me first explain what is *not* under discussion in this book. First, I will not take time to defend the reality of hell. Instead, I take for granted that hell is real, mainly because this seems obvious from the Old and New Testament scriptures. Secondly, I will not defend a view on exactly *who* goes to hell or what the necessary or sufficient conditions are for avoiding damnation. This book is not an inquiry into the moral-epistemic criteria for salvation. Thirdly, I will not defend a particular view regarding *why* people go to hell. While Christians generally agree that hell is a result of people's sinful rebellion against God, some see hell as a means of *retributive punishment* for this rebellion (e.g., Thomas Aquinas and Jonathan Edwards) while others (e.g., Jonathan Kvanvig and Eleonore Stump) conceive of hell as a *natural consequence* of rejecting God. I believe both of these views to be insightful and do not see them as mutually exclusive.

Fourthly, I will not defend a view on exactly what hell involves (e.g., literal burning, psychological torment, etc.). I assume here only that hell is a very distressing and undesirable state of being. This rules out so-called "mild" and "moderate" views of hell, which have been suggested by some scholars.[2] Most Christian theologians agree that hell involves some sort of separation from God. For example, Thomas Oden asserts that "exclusion from the presence of God is the central meaning of hell."[3] This basic idea has been affirmed in the Fourth Lateran Council, the Quicunque Creed, the Council of Valence III, among others, and it is consistent with all three of the major views of hell to be discussed. I would only add to this an emphasis on the point that such separation from God causes the damned to

---

2. See, for example, Brown and Walls, "Annihilationism," 56; Crisp, "Divine Retribution," 46; and Bawulski, "Annihilationism," 75–78.

3. Oden, *Life in the Spirit*, 450.

experience deep distress or torment, as also seems clear from several passages of Scripture (e.g., Matt 5:22; Mark 9:43–47; Luke 16:23–28; 2 Pet 2:4; Rev 14:10–11; 20:10).

The main questions under consideration here are (1) whether the experience of hell is everlasting or finite in duration and (2) if the torments of hell have a termination, whether the experience of hell is followed by annihilation or restoration to God. My overarching thesis is that, all things considered, conditionalism seems most likely to be true. Each of the three views enjoys some significant biblical evidential warrant while each also faces some serious biblical objections. It is for this reason that the issue merits close *philosophical* investigation. It is my view that such a philosophical inquiry points rather decisively against the traditional view and, to a lesser extent, against universalism.

This book is primarily a philosophical inquiry into the subject of hell, but because it is an inherently theological topic, the philosophical analysis requires a biblical textual foundation.[4] I provide this in chapter 1, where I canvass the major scriptural arguments for and against each of the three views of hell. I conclude that, all things considered, conditionalism enjoys the most biblical warrant. The next two chapters mainly subject the traditional view to critique. Chapter 2 focuses on the question of justice and concludes that the doctrine of eternal conscious torment presents tremendous difficulties from the standpoint of justice, while conditionalism and universalism face no significant difficulties when it comes to the matter of justice. Chapter 3 addresses the problem of evil as it relates to the doctrine of hell. I compare the three views of hell in terms of how the two leading responses to the problem of evil—the free-will defense and the soul-making theodicy—may be applied in the context of each view. I conclude that neither approach is of any help to traditionalism and that the problem of evil is most severe for this view.

The last two chapters are concerned with critiquing universalism and rebutting some major arguments for universalism. Chapter 4 explores some arguments aimed at showing that human beings are naturally immortal, and I show why each of these fails. Next I discuss five different arguments that have been used to refute universalism and conclude that three of these do succeed in undercutting the view. These concern problems for the

---

4. This is essentially a caveat for those who might be primarily interested in a biblical-theological treatment of the issue. There are plenty of other resources for that, many of which will be cited throughout the discussion.

universalist related to human freedom, divine freedom, and the meaning of salvation. Finally, chapter 5 addresses what I call the problem of heavenly grief—the objection to non-universalist views on the grounds that they entail that the redeemed in heaven cannot be truly happy because of the suffering of the damned. I identify serious problems with a variety of approaches to solving this problem and then offer my own original solution, which I believe effectively defeats the universalist's appeal to the problem of heavenly grief as a means of defending their view.

The book, then, is essentially a comparative defense of conditionalism, which can be summed up as follows. Conditionalism enjoys more biblical warrant than traditionalism and universalism. And conditionalism is far more defensible philosophically than traditionalism and somewhat more defensible philosophically than universalism. Specifically, the traditional view of hell is deeply problematic when it comes to the matter of justice and the problem of evil. Universalism is probably the least problematic among the three views regarding the problem of evil, but the problems with universalism identified in chapter 4—regarding human freedom, divine freedom, and the meaning of salvation—more than offset any philosophical advantage that might be enjoyed by universalism. The upshot, then, is that conditionalism is, all things considered, the most defensible view of hell among the three major alternatives.

A TERMINOLOGICAL CLARIFICATION

As noted, my designation for the view I defend in this book is "conditional immortality." This refers to the idea that human beings do not naturally live forever, at least since the fall, and that immortality is part of the gift of salvation in Christ. While the view often goes under the name "annihilationism," I hesitate to use the term because this sometimes invites confusion regarding what the doctrine actually entails. Thus, some take "annihilationism" to mean that the wicked are immediately destroyed after the last judgment so they never experience the torments of hell. I have found that use of "conditional immortality" or "conditionalism" tends to preclude this misunderstanding, even if there are potential problems with this terminology as well. For example, Clark Pinnock complains that the conditional nature of our immortality is only a necessary, not a sufficient condition, for the annihilation of the wicked, because "it would still be possible that God might give the wicked everlasting life and condemn them to spend it

Introduction

in everlasting torment."[5] However, I am not convinced that this bare logical possibility provides grounds to worry about any potential confusion that the view might allow for eternal conscious torment.

Some who affirm the annihilation of the wicked opt for still other terminology. John Stackhouse prefers the appellation "terminal punishment" for his view that "hell is the situation in which those who do not avail themselves of the atonement made by Jesus in his suffering and death must make their own atonement by suffering and then death, separated from the sustaining life of God and thus disappearing from the cosmos."[6] While I respect Stackhouse's terminological choice, I don't like the vagueness of the term, since we normally associate "terminal" with earthly death, rather than death of the soul, whereas "conditional immortality" clearly pertains to the post-mortem state. Moreover, the term "punishment" in Stackhouse's name for the view commits one to the idea that annihilation of the soul is part of the penalty for sin. In contrast, "conditional immortality" leaves the matter open, which is a desirable thing since conditionalists disagree among one another on whether annihilation is part of the punishment of the wicked or simply a natural consequence of their not receiving the gift of immortality.

Whatever difficulties might attend use of the terms "conditional immortality" or "conditionalism," I am content with this terminology. After all, similar quibbles could be made regarding the terms "traditionalism" and "universalism," both of which fail to capture important aspects of these views. Anyway, one should not expect too much from a short name for an entire doctrine. The important thing is that the doctrine itself is reasonable, both from a biblical and philosophical standpoint. At least that is what I intend to show.

---

5. Pinnock, "Destruction," 67.
6. Stackhouse, "Terminal Punishment," 61–62.

1

Biblical Considerations

As we saw in the introduction, the concept of hell as eternal conscious torment has been the preeminent view since St. Augustine. Yet the early church was deeply divided on the matter. In the first few centuries of Christian history, leading theologians and biblical scholars can be found on all sides of the debate. This probably explains why we find no early creedal statement specifying a particular view on the doctrine, except to affirm the reality of hell. Division in the early church over the issue is understandable considering the biblical arguments that can be mustered in defense of each of the three major views on hell. It is the purpose of this chapter to review the biblical texts most relevant to this debate. This is crucial for our purposes, most obviously because this book is a work in philosophical theology, and many of the passages discussed will be brought back into focus in later chapters. Furthermore, this review of biblical texts is also important because, as I hope will become evident, even careful biblical and systematic theology cannot adequately decide the debate over hell. Hence, this will underscore the need for philosophical inquiry to augment and enhance our understanding of the issues and perhaps lead us to a decisive conclusion on the subject.

THE TRADITIONAL VIEW

Let us begin with the principal texts supporting the traditional view of hell as eternal conscious torment. Biblical scholars such as Robert Peterson and Denny Burk routinely appeal to ten biblical passages that they claim support this view.[1] One of these is Isaiah 66:22–24, which provides this eschatological message:

> "As the new heavens and the new earth that I make will endure before me," declares the Lord, "so will your name and descendants endure. From one New Moon to another and from one Sabbath to another, all mankind will come and bow down before me," says the Lord. "And they will go out and look on the dead bodies of those who rebelled against me; the worms that eat them will not die, the fire that burns them will not be quenched, and they will be loathsome to all mankind."[2]

Here Isaiah describes the final state of the righteous and the wicked. Note that the fate of the wicked is punitive, not redemptive. And it appears that the punishment is everlasting, given that "the worms that eat them will not die" and "the fire that burns them will not be quenched." After all, maggots and fire would not continue to consume a body if that body has been annihilated (if conditionalism is true) or finally redeemed (if universalism is true). Thus, as Denny Burk puts it, "this scene seems to assume that God's enemies have been given a body fit for an unending punishment."[3] But whether or not the punishment is corporal, traditionalists insist that what this passage indicates is an everlasting torment. As John Calvin remarks about this text, "the plain meaning . . . is that the wicked shall have a bad conscience as an executioner, to torment them without end, and that torment awaits them greater than all other torments."[4] But is this really a fair assumption? The reference to undying worms and unquenchable fire may just as well indicate that (1) their devouring and burning cannot be stopped and (2) what they are devouring and burning will be completely destroyed. Even universalism does not appear to be ruled out by this passage, as an omnipotent God has the power to eventually rescue the wicked from the otherwise irresistible destructive action of the worms and fire, perhaps after hundreds or thousands of years of torment.

Another key Old Testament passage is Daniel 12:1–2: "At that time Michael, the great prince who protects your people, will arise. There will

---

1. See Peterson, "Case for Traditionalism" and Burk, "Eternal Conscious Torment."
2. This and all other scriptural quotes are from the New International Version of the Bible.
3. Burk, "Eternal Conscious Torment," 23.
4. Calvin, *Prophet Isaiah*, 439.

be a time of distress such as has not happened from the beginning of nations until then. But at that time your people—everyone whose name is found written in the book—will be delivered. Multitudes who sleep in the dust of the earth will awake: some to everlasting life, others to shame and everlasting contempt." Like the Isaiah passage, here we have a vivid contrast between the fates of the righteous and the wicked, who will arise to "everlasting life" and "everlasting contempt," respectively. The parallel use of the term "everlasting" suggests that, like the righteous, the damned will live forever, only in a condition of shame. But, as with the Isaiah passage, we must be careful not to read into the text what is not there. For contempt itself does not necessitate conscious experience. The Hebrew term here translated as "contempt"—the same term translated as "loathsome" in Isaiah 66:24—refers to that which is an object of abhorrence or aversion,[5] and this does not imply consciousness on the part of what is abhorred. As John Stackhouse notes, "this text says literally nothing about whether the damned are conscious forever to be ashamed of their contemptible reputations. Their reputations live on in ignominy, so to speak, whether they are alive or dead. That's all Daniel is saying."[6] Thus, to resist the traditionalist interpretation of this passage, the conditionalist need not challenge the claim that the fate of the wicked is everlasting. She need only reject the assumption that what lasts forever is their conscious torment.

Turning to the New Testament, we find Jesus using rather strong eschatological language in the Gospel texts. One of these passages is Matthew 18:8–9, where Jesus declares, "If your hand or your foot causes you to stumble, cut it off and throw it away. It is better for you to enter life maimed or crippled than to have two hands or two feet and be thrown into eternal fire. And if your eye causes you to stumble, gouge it out and throw it away. It is better for you to enter life with one eye than to have two eyes and be thrown into the fire of hell." Here we find Jesus recycling a hyperbolic statement he makes in Matthew 5 regarding gouging out an eye or cutting off a hand that causes one to stumble. In both passages he concludes with a warning about hell, but here he reinforces the point by contrasting the fates of the repentant and unrepentant, where the latter are "thrown into the fire of hell." The word rendered as "hell" here is historically significant. The Greek word (*geenna*) derives from the Hebrew term (*ge hinnom*), meaning "Valley of Hinnom," which is where worshipers of Molech sacrificed children

---

5. See Miller, *Daniel*, 317.
6. Stackhouse, "Terminal Punishment Response," 47.

Biblical Considerations

and where, according to the prophet Jeremiah, the wrath of God would be visited on these wicked idolaters, such that it would be known as the "Valley of Slaughter" (Jer 7:31–34). So, as with the Isaiah and Daniel passages, the fate of the wicked here seems punitive, rather than restorative. And the contrast between the "life" awaiting the righteous and the "eternal fire" that awaits the wicked suggests that both fates are everlasting. However, again, nothing in the texts explicitly indicates that the doomed last forever in the fire, much less that they suffer everlasting conscious torment. Nor does the text rule out the possibility of eventual redemption from the fiery fate.

Another popular traditionalist text appears later in the same Gospel—Matthew 25:31–46:

> When the Son of Man comes in his glory, and all the angels with him, he will sit on his glorious throne. All the nations will be gathered before him, and he will separate the people one from another as a shepherd separates the sheep from the goats. He will put the sheep on his right and the goats on his left.
>
> Then the King will say to those on his right, "Come, you who are blessed by my Father; take your inheritance, the kingdom prepared for you since the creation of the world." . . .
>
> Then he will say to those on his left, "Depart from me, you who are cursed, into the eternal fire prepared for the devil and his angels . . ."
>
> Then they will go away to eternal punishment, but the righteous to eternal life.

Here we have yet another sharp contrast between the wicked and righteous, accentuated by the use of parallel expressions—"eternal punishment" and "eternal life." As with the Daniel passage, traditionalists regard this as indicating that both the wicked and righteous will live forever. This reasoning dates at least as far back as Augustine, who said, "what a fond fancy is it to suppose that eternal punishment means long-continued punishment, while eternal life means life without end . . . . If both destinies are 'eternal,' then we must either understand both as long-continued but at last terminating, or both as endless."[7]

Two responses to Augustine's argument are appropriate here. First, the term translated as "eternal" in this passage, as well as in Matthew 18:8, is *aiōnios*. This adjective indicates some kind of relationship to "an age" (from the noun *aiōn*, referring to a period of time, an age). In this period *aiōn*

---

7. Augustine, *City of God*, 793.

could be shorthand in some Jewish writings for a very specific age—i.e., "the age to come"— and *aiōnios* could function as an adjective referring to that same "age." Thus, *aiōnios* punishment is age-to-come punishment. It need not be everlasting but might rather merely indicate a very long period of suffering. Thus, A. W. Argyle interprets "eternal punishment" as meaning "punishment characteristic of the Age to come" and "eternal life" as "the life that belongs to the Age to come, the full abundant life which is fellowship with God."[8] Secondly, even if *aiōnios* is interpreted as "everlasting," thus indicating that the punishment of the wicked lasts forever, this does not imply that the torment of the damned is everlasting. Instead, it may be that their final destruction is permanent. Thus, as Edward Fudge puts it, "once destroyed, the wicked will never be seen again. The *result* is everlasting, not the *process*."[9]

In the Gospel of Mark we find the following passage, which is a parallel text to the Matthew 18 passage discussed above: "If your foot causes you to stumble, cut it off. It is better for you to enter life crippled than to have two feet and be thrown into hell. And if your eye causes you to stumble, pluck it out. It is better for you to enter the kingdom of God with one eye than to have two eyes and be thrown into hell, where 'the worms that eat them do not die, and the fire is not quenched'" (Mark 9:45–48). Note here Jesus' inclusion of the worm and fire imagery from Isaiah 66. Our observations regarding the implications of those images in the Isaiah passage apply here as well. The images of undying worms and unquenchable fire are indeed consistent with the idea of everlasting torment of the damned, but such an interpretation is not necessary, as it is also consistent with the concept of complete and unstoppable destruction of the damned.

Among the Pauline texts, the most significant passage related to the hell debate is 2 Thessalonians 1:8–10: "[God] will punish those who do not know God and do not obey the gospel of our Lord Jesus. They will be punished with everlasting destruction and shut out from the presence of the Lord and from the glory of his might on the day he comes to be glorified in his holy people and to be marveled at among all those who have believed." Here, again, the purpose of the promised punishment is retribution rather than rehabilitation. And, of course, the key phrase is "everlasting destruction." The sense of the Greek term translated as destruction (*oletheros*) is utter loss or complete ruin, and parties to the debate disagree over exactly

8. Argyle, *Gospel According to Matthew*, 193.
9. Fudge, "Case for Conditionalism," 59.

Biblical Considerations

what this implies regarding the fate of the damned. Traditionalists conceive destruction in this context as an ongoing process of devastation.[10] Conditionalists, on the other hand, insist that true destruction has a terminus, and it is the *finality* of the annihilation of the wicked that is everlasting, not the process of destroying. After all, if the destruction is always in process, can we say that the wicked are ever truly destroyed? In any case, when it comes to interpreting the meaning of the phrase "everlasting destruction," these are the two most natural options. Universalists usually appeal to a more strained reading, such as the notion that what is permanently destroyed in hell is people's wickedness, not people themselves.

The phrase "shut out from the presence of the Lord" is also significant. Traditionalists maintain that to be "shut out" implies that one is barred from entry, not that one is extinguished. Howard Marshall raises the point that "separation from the Lord is of little significance if those punished are not conscious of their separation."[11] Conditionalists such as Edward Fudge, however, point out that since God is omnipresent, the only way one could be shut out from God's presence is to be annihilated and thus no longer exist.[12] Meanwhile, universalists propose that this shutting out of the wicked is specifiable to a particular time (the day Christ "comes to be glorified in his holy people . . .") and thus need not be interpreted as a permanent condition of the wicked.

Although the book of Jude is a short book, it has a lot to say about the fate of the ungodly. After some encouraging opening words, in verses 5–7 we read:

> Though you already know all this, I want to remind you that the Lord at one time delivered his people out of Egypt, but later destroyed those who did not believe. And the angels who did not keep their positions of authority but abandoned their proper dwelling—these he has kept in darkness, bound with everlasting chains for judgment on the great Day. In a similar way, Sodom and Gomorrah and the surrounding towns gave themselves up to

---

10. For example, regarding New Testament references to the destruction of the wicked, Wayne Grudem says "the terms used for 'destruction' do not necessarily imply a ceasing to exist or some kind of annihilation, but can simply be ways of referring to the harmful and destructive effects of final judgment on unbelievers" (*Systematic Theology*, 1150).

11. Marshall, *1 and 2 Thessalonians*, 179.

12. Fudge, *Fire that Consumes*, 249n36.

> sexual immorality and perversion. They serve as an example of those who suffer the punishment of eternal fire.

And a few verses later, the writer says "They are wild waves of the sea, foaming up their shame; wandering stars, for whom blackest darkness has been reserved forever" (v. 13). There is that phrase "eternal fire" again, and as we've seen, this may or may not entail everlasting "burning" of the wicked. The fire might only be "eternal" (*aiōnios*) in the sense of long-lasting, and even if it is everlasting fire, this doesn't imply that those who are subject to it remain conscious forever. The wicked might be annihilated by that fire, as conditionalists maintain is suggested by the writer's comparison to Sodom and Gomorrah, which were completely *extinguished* by the fire of God. Or the wicked might ultimately be rescued from the fire, as universalists contend.

As for the "blackest darkness" that "has been reserved forever" for the wicked, this also seems compatible with all three perspectives. Although this darkness has been "reserved forever," this doesn't entail that those who are subject to it remain there perpetually. Eternal conscious torment in that condition is possible, but it is also possible that the damned are consigned to this darkness for a long but finite period, then annihilated or finally rescued and redeemed.

The most troubling biblical texts for non-traditionalists appear in the book of Revelation. One of these is Revelation 14:9–11:

> A third angel followed them and said in a loud voice: "If anyone worships the beast and its image and receives its mark on their forehead or on their hand, they, too, will drink the wine of God's fury, which has been poured full strength into the cup of his wrath. They will be tormented with burning sulfur in the presence of the holy angels and of the Lamb. And the smoke of their torment will rise for ever and ever. There will be no rest day or night for those who worship the beast and its image, or for anyone who receives the mark of its name."

First, regarding the phrase "no rest day or night," this indicates that the suffering of those tormented will be relentless for as long as it lasts, though the expression itself gives no indication of the duration of the suffering. But what exactly does John mean when he says "the smoke of their torment will rise forever and ever"? Traditionalists argue that this implies the everlasting torment of the damned because it is not merely the smoke from the burning of the damned that perpetually rises but rather specifically the smoke of their *torment*, thus suggesting that the wicked suffer endlessly. After all, as Gregory Beale notes, "annihilation would be a kind of rest or relief from the excruciating torment of the brief final judgement," hence the damned must suffer an "ongoing torment of restlessness."[13] Non-traditionalists observe, however, that the torment of the damned and the rising smoke that signifies that torment are nonetheless distinct things, and the latter may linger even while the former has ceased. Conditionalists in particular are quick to point out that in this passage John is actually quoting Isaiah 34:9–10, which concerns Edom and alludes to the complete destruction of Sodom and Gomorrah in Genesis 19, where the smoke that "will rise forever" indicates utter *destruction* of the cities. In the case of Edom in Isaiah 34, the "smoke will rise forever," though the kingdom is utterly destroyed.[14]

The final pro-traditionalist passage is Revelation 20:10, 14–15: "the devil . . . was thrown into the lake of burning sulfur, where the beast and the false prophet had been thrown. They will be tormented day and night for ever and ever. . . . Then death and Hades were thrown into the lake of fire. The lake of fire is the second death. Anyone whose name was not found written in the book of life was thrown into the lake of fire." It does appear from verse 10 that those who are thrown into the lake of fire suffer eternal conscious torment. But it is important to note that the devil, beast, and false prophet are not human beings. In fact, many biblical scholars interpret the "beast" and "false prophet" as institutions or abstract entities, rather than individual conscious beings. Thus, Fudge says the beast and false prophet are "representations of persecuting civil government and of corrupting false religion. Neither institution will be perpetuated forever, nor could either suffer conscious, sensible pain."[15] Fudge, however, does not specifically challenge the standard orthodox view that the devil is a conscious, personal being. And if the devil suffers eternal conscious torment in the lake of fire, then it seems appropriate to conclude that humans who are cast there also suffer eternally. Or, if the devil is unlike human beings in so far as he suffers eternally while humans do not, then this presents a justice problem for the conditionalist. For although the devil's sins may be far greater than those of any human, they are nonetheless finite and thus not deserving of endless

---

13. Beale, *Book of Revelation*, 764.

14. For a detailed analysis of this passage supporting a conditionalist perspective, see Bowles, "Revelation 14:11."

15. Fudge, *Fire that Consumes*, 303.

torment, that is if one grants that humans should be spared endless torment for the same reason.

THE CONDITIONALIST VIEW

As we have seen, in support of their claim that the torment of the damned lasts forever, traditionalists appeal to use of the word "eternal" (*aiōnios*) in Matthew 25:46 and 2 Thessalonians 1:9. Biblical scholars disagree as to exactly how the term is properly to be understood, with some insisting that it refers to an age of unknown duration, while others, including conditionalist theologian Edward Fudge, interpret the term as implying everlasting duration.[16] Whichever meaning is assigned to the term, conditionalism does not appear to be threatened by these passages. If *aiōnios* is read as a fixed temporal duration (an age or ages), then obviously the punishment (Matt 25:46) or destruction (2 Thess 1:9) of the wicked in hell need not be regarded as everlasting. But even if *aiōnios* is understood in the sense of unending in these passages, the question remains exactly *what* lasts forever—the *torment* of those being punished/destroyed or the *consequence* of that punishment/destruction.

It is important to note that six times in the New Testament *aiōnios* functions as an adjective modifying a term of action. Two of these instances are the passages under consideration (Matt 25:46 and 2 Thess 1:9), where *aiōnios* modifies "punishment" and "destruction." But in each of the other four New Testament uses, *aiōnios* describes not an endless *process* but an endless *result* of a finite process. These include the *eternal sin* that is blasphemy of the Holy Spirit (Mark 3:29), the *eternal judgment* referenced by the writer of Hebrews (Heb 6:2), our *eternal redemption* achieved through Christ's atoning work (Heb 9:12), and the *eternal salvation* awaiting all those who are faithfully obedient to Christ (Heb 5:9). In each of these cases, *aiōnios* signifies an everlasting result of a finite process. So it is consistent with New Testament usage to interpret the use of *aiōnios* in Matthew 25:46 and 2 Thessalonians 1:9 in similar fashion. In the latter case, the destruction is finitely achieved, but its effect—the extinction of the damned—is permanent and unending. And in the former, as Fudge puts it, "the punish*ing*

---

16. Fudge interprets *aiōnios* as referring to "unlimited time within the limits determined by the limits of the thing it modifies" (*Fire that Consumes*, 40).

continues until the process is completed, and then it stops. But the *punishment* which results will remain forever."[17]

Now suppose that in these passages we interpret *aiōnios* in the sense of a fixed duration (age or ages). Some traditionalists object that this undermines our confidence in the biblical promise of eternal life for the redeemed. This is a misguided objection, however, since there are numerous biblical passages reinforcing the doctrine of everlasting life for Christians which do not involve the term *aiōnios*. For instance, in Romans 8:38-39 Paul says believers will never be separated from the love of God. In 1 Thessalonians 4:17, he says we will "always" (*pantote*) "be with the Lord." In 1 Timothy 10 and 1 Corinthians 15, Paul notes that Christians have been given immortality through the work of Christ. Peter tells us that Christians have an inheritance in heaven "that can never perish, spoil or fade" (1 Pet 1:4), and later in the same book he says we will "receive the crown of glory that will never fade away" (1 Pet 5:4). And in the book of Revelation, we are promised that when we dwell with God in the new heaven and new earth "there will be no more death" (21:4). Furthermore, a *theological* foundation for everlasting life is grounded in the fact that such life is a participation in Christ's resurrection life, which is imperishable. There is no such theological foundation for eternal torment. All of this shows that Christians have overwhelming biblical grounds to be confident that they will live forever with God, regardless of how *aiōnios* is interpreted in New Testament texts.

Biblical Imagery of Fire

Now as for positive arguments for conditional immortality, or "terminal punishment" as Stackhouse prefers to call it, there are numerous biblical passages that appear to support this view. I will categorize these passages under the topical headings of the biblical imagery of fire, the biblical language of destruction, and the biblical theme of opposing life and death. Beginning with the first theme, Scripture tells us that God is a "consuming fire" (Deut 4:24; Heb 12:29), which is unquenchable (Ezek 20:47-48) and reduces to nothing whatever is subject to it (Amos 5:5-6). The prophet Isaiah says the wicked "will be burned to ashes; like cut thornbushes they will be set ablaze" (Isa 33:12). The prophet Malachi announces the coming fate of the wicked as being subjected to a furnace so that "'all the arrogant and every evildoer will be stubble, and the day that is coming will set them on

17. Fudge, *Fire that Consumes*, 48.

fire,' says the LORD Almighty. 'Not a root or a branch will be left to them. . . . Then you will trample on the wicked; they will be ashes under the soles of your feet,'" (Mal 4:1, 3).

As for the nature of hell, Scripture repeatedly describes this with imagery of fire. Jesus declares that at the end of the age "angels will come and separate the wicked from the righteous and throw them into the blazing furnace, where there will be weeping and gnashing of teeth" (Matt 13:49–50). In Matthew, as noted above, Jesus refers to the "fire of hell" (18:9), and as an "eternal fire" (Matt 18:8 and 25:41). In the Gospel of Mark, hearkening back to the language of Isaiah 66, Jesus refers to the fire of hell as unquenchable (Mark 9:43, 48). As noted above, this might as easily be read to confirm conditionalism as the traditional view of hell. Basil Atkinson writes, "unquenchable fire in scripture is . . . fire that cannot be put out until it has totally devoured what it was kindled to burn up. Such will be the fire that will burn up the wicked."[18]

In the book of Revelation there are multiple references to the fire of divine wrath. As we noted already, in chapter 14, those who worship the beast "will be tormented with burning sulfur" (v. 10). Later in the book of Revelation we are told about the "lake of fire" where the devil, the beast, and the false prophet will burn (Rev 19:20; 20:10), where death and Hades will be thrown (Rev 20:14). And not just them but also "the cowardly, the unbelieving, the vile, the murderers, the sexually immoral, those who practice magic arts, the idolaters and all liars—they will be consigned to the fiery lake of burning sulfur. This is the second death" (Rev 21:8).

As many conditionalists have noted, such imagery suggests complete annihilation, as fire consumes and totally destroys what it burns. However, traditionalists and universalists counter with the observation that destruction is not the only purpose or effect of fire. Such imagery also serves to suggest painful torment, which, traditionalists are correct to point out, could continue indefinitely. Fire also is serviceable for purification purposes, as is frequently noted by restorationist universalists, who regard hell as God's final means of drawing the unrepentant back to himself.

---

18. Atkinson, "Doom of the Lost," 108. Harold E. Guillebaud also has the following to say about this terminology: "The word 'unquenchable' means simply 'that which nothing and no one can quench,' which cannot be prevented from accomplishing its destructive purpose. But there may be the further thought that, after it has completed the destruction, it continues forever as a memorial of the wrath of God" ("General Trend," 157).

Biblical Considerations

Biblical Language of Destruction

Repeatedly throughout Scripture, the fate of the wicked is depicted and described as that of utter destruction.[19] The most vivid Old Testament narrative of divine wrath is that of the annihilation of Sodom and Gomorrah (Gen 19). It is noteworthy that the apostle Peter declares that God "made them an example of what is going to happen to the ungodly" (2 Pet 2:6). When Abraham looked upon the plain where those two cities once stood, he "saw dense smoke rising from the land, like smoke from a furnace" (Gen 19:28), a visible testament to the complete destruction of those wicked people. In parallel fashion, we are told in Revelation 14 regarding those who are subjected to God's final fury that "the smoke of their torment will rise for ever and ever"—again, an image of final destruction.

The Psalms frequently refer to the fact that the wicked will be utterly destroyed. One psalmist compares the perishing of the wicked to wax melting before the fire (Ps 68:2). In Psalm 1, we read that the wicked "are like chaff that the wind blows away. Therefore the wicked will not stand in the judgment, nor sinners in the assembly of the righteous. For the Lord watches over the way of the righteous, but the way of the wicked leads to destruction" (vv. 4–6). Psalm 37 tells us that those who are evil will wither like grass and "like green plants they will soon die away" (v. 2), that soon the "wicked will be no more; though you look for them, they will not be found" (v. 10). And a few verses later: "the wicked will perish . . . they will be consumed, they will go up in smoke" (v. 20).

The same theme of utter destruction is echoed throughout Proverbs, as "the wicked are overthrown and are no more" (Prov 12:7), and "the evildoer has no future hope . . . the lamp of the wicked will be snuffed out" (Prov 24:20). The prophet Isaiah says, "Do not fear the reproach of mere mortals or be terrified by their insults. For the moth will eat them up like a garment; the worm will devour them like wool" (Isa 51:7–8). These and many other passages depict the complete destruction of the wicked.

In the New Testament, too, we find emphatic language of destruction in reference to the damned. Paul asserts that the wicked "will be punished with everlasting destruction and shut out from the presence of the Lord

---

19. For a summary review and categorization of all of the biblical references to the fate of the lost, see Wenham, "Case for Conditional Immortality," 79–82. Wenham finds 264 such references, and in all but one of these (Rev 14:11) "there is not a word about unending torment and very many of them in their natural sense clearly refer to destruction" (p. 82).

Hell and Divine Goodness

and from the majesty of his power" (2 Thess 1:9). And the destruction of the soul in hell is referenced specifically by Jesus, when he says, "do not be afraid of those who kill the body but cannot kill the soul. Rather, be afraid of the one who can destroy both soul and body in hell" (Matt 10:28). In regards to this passage, John Stott observes, "it would seem strange . . . if people who are said to suffer destruction are not in fact destroyed."[20]

Finally, the biblical concept of the destruction of the wicked extends even to the point of extinguishing the memory of them. The psalmist declares of the wicked, "Surely you place them on slippery ground; you cast them down to ruin. How suddenly are they destroyed, completely swept away by terrors! They are like a dream when one awakes; when you arise, Lord, you will despise them as fantasies" (Ps 73:20). Another psalmist puts it even more strongly: "You have rebuked the nations and destroyed the wicked; you have blotted out their name for ever and ever. Endless ruin has overtaken the enemy, you have uprooted their cities; even the memory of them has perished" (Ps 9:5–6).

Clearly, the destruction of the wicked is a strong scriptural theme.[21] But does this really entail annihilation of the damned? Traditionalists insist that we need not make this inference, since, in ordinary conversation, destruction often means utter loss, as opposed to extinction of being. Reinforcing this point, the Greek term *olethron*, translated as "destruction" in such passages as 2 Thessalonians 1:9, often means "ruin," depending on the context. Thus, Denny Burk says, "if I were to say that my car was destroyed in a crash last week, no one hears that to mean that the car ceases to exist. They understand it to mean that the car was completely ruined and lost to me as a result of the accident."[22] So, according to Burk, the destruction of the damned consists in their permanent alienation from the Lord. While this interpretation might work with some biblical passages, it is difficult to square Burk's approach with others, especially those that declare that even the memory of the wicked will be no more (Ps 9:6), that the wicked will be completely consumed and despised as mere "fantasies" (Ps 73:20) and reduced to mere ashes (Mal 4:3).

Universalists push back by noting that there is a reasonable sense of temporary destruction, such as is evident in the analogy of a city that is

---

20. Stott, "Judgment and Hell," 51.

21. For a fuller discussion of this biblical theme and its implications for the doctrine of hell, see Pinnock, "Destruction," 63–65.

22. Burk, "Eternal Conscious Torment," 35.

completely destroyed and then rebuilt. If a city can be restored after its total destruction, then why can't the same be true of a human being, including those who are cast into hell? But there are a couple of problems with this approach. First, such a view cannot account for the biblical notion that the destruction of the wicked in hell is "everlasting" (2 Thess 1:9). Nor can it account for the recurrent contrast between those who are destroyed and those who are saved (e.g., Phil 1:28; Heb 10:39). Such a contrast is inappropriate if those who are destroyed are also ultimately saved as well.

Another potential route of response for the universalist in making sense of the destruction of the damned may be to insist that what is permanently destroyed in hell is not the person as a whole (on conditionalism) or even their fellowship with God (on traditionalism) but rather all of their negative qualities and sinful dispositions. In short, the destruction of the wicked in hell pertains only to the wicked*ness* of the damned. It is just the utter destruction of their evil that is everlasting. However, this approach, too, fails to properly distinguish the damned from the saved, since it is also the case for the saved that their sinfulness will be destroyed. In fact, this is the distinguishing feature of the redeemed in Christ—that our sins are wiped away completely (i.e., destroyed), and herein lies the means of our salvation and eternal life. So if the universalist appeals to this same thing (the obliteration of our sinfulness) as the essence of the destruction of the damned, then this undermines the entire distinction between the saved and the damned that we find permeating the pages of Scripture.[23]

Biblical Opposition of Life and Death

Throughout Scripture, we find a consistent contrast between life and death as the respective destinies of the righteous and the wicked. This begins in the opening chapters of Genesis where the first humans are warned that if they eat from the tree of knowledge of good and evil, they "will certainly die" (Gen 2:17). The consequence of their disobedience, of course, was not mere physical mortality, but rather a "second death," which follows the death of the body (Rev 20:14; 21:8). Since the fall of humankind, conditionalists argue, immortality is a gracious gift from God, as Paul seems to

---

23. Robin Parry (pseudonymously published as Gregory MacDonald) deploys both of these strategies in addressing the conditionalist argument from destruction. See *Evangelical Universalist*, 151–55.

Hell and Divine Goodness

indicate when he says, "the perishable must clothe itself with the imperishable, and the mortal with immortality" (1 Cor 15:53).

Elsewhere in Scripture, there are reiterations of the theme that the reward for the righteous is life everlasting, while the promised fate of the wicked is death. A proverb says, "in the way of righteousness there is life; along that path is immortality" (Prov 12:28). And the apostle John succinctly juxtaposes the fates of the saved and the lost, in noting that "whoever believes in [Christ] shall not perish but have eternal life" (John 3:16). Jesus also says, "enter through the narrow gate. For wide is the gate and broad is the road that leads to destruction, and many people enter through it. But small is the gate and narrow the road that leads to life, and only a few find it" (Matt 7:13–14). In these passages the reward for the righteous is immortality or everlasting life, the implication being that the way of the wicked leads to the opposite of this, the discontinuation of life or death of the soul.

The language of opposition between life and death is especially prevalent in the Pauline literature. In the book of Romans Paul draws a sharp contrast between the consequences of the life of sin and the life of righteousness:

> When you were slaves to sin, you were free from the control of righteousness. What benefit did you reap at that time from the things you are now ashamed of? Those things result in death! But now that you have been set free from sin and have become slaves to God, the benefit you reap leads to holiness, and the result is eternal life.
>
> (Rom. 6:20–22)

Elsewhere, Paul says, "The one who sows to please his sinful nature, from that nature will reap destruction; the one who sows to please the Spirit, from the Spirit will reap eternal life" (Gal 6:8). And in Philippians, he counsels his readers not to fear those who hate them, as "This is a sign to them that they will be destroyed, but that you will be saved" (Phil 1:28). In short, Paul's point in each of these passages is that the life of sin brings death, while righteousness in Christ brings "eternal life." Such a distinction makes little sense if the traditional or universalist view of hell is correct, since they affirm that everyone lives forever anyway. On the traditional view, there is eternal life for everyone, though the quality of the life of the damned is torturous. And for the universalist, everyone ultimately experiences everlasting salvific joy. In the Pauline literature, it appears all that is everlasting for the damned is their "destruction" (2 Thess 1:9).

Regarding this ubiquitous Scriptural theme of life-death opposition, both traditionalists and universalists are inclined to insist that death is not extinction of being but rather separation from God. Thus, Robert Peterson proposes that, "as death means the separation of the soul from the body, so the second death denotes the ultimate separation of the ungodly from God's love."[24] For the traditionalist, this is an everlasting conscious separation of the wicked from God's love, while for the universalist it is only a temporary condition that ultimately leads to or is followed by redemption.

THE UNIVERSALIST VIEW

The case for universalism begins with the Abrahamic covenant, where the Lord declares to Abram that "all peoples on earth will be blessed through you" (Gen 12:3). Just as the nation of Israel was God's elect people by whom he would bring the other nations to salvation, so God has chosen his church in the Christian era to be his vehicle of salvation for the whole world. The question, of course, is whether God's salvific plan will ultimately achieve salvation for everyone.

Reconciling All Things to Himself: Colossians 1:15–20

One text which does appear to suggest that God will achieve universal salvation, not only for all human beings but for all other creatures as well, is found in Colossians 1:

> The Son is the image of the invisible God, the firstborn over all creation. For in him all things were created: things in heaven and on earth, visible and invisible, whether thrones or powers or rulers or authorities; all things have been created through him and for him. He is before all things, and in him all things hold together. And he is the head of the body, the church; he is the beginning and the firstborn from among the dead, so that in everything he

---

24. Peterson, "Case for Traditionalism," 165. Here, Peterson follows a long line of theologians, including W. G. T. Shedd, who maintained, "in spiritual death the soul is separated from God, as in physical death the soul is separated from the body. The union of the soul with God is spiritual life; its separation from God is spiritual death" (*Dogmatic Theology*, 898).

might have the supremacy. For God was pleased to have all his fullness dwell in him, and through him to reconcile to himself all things, whether things on earth or things in heaven, by making peace through his blood, shed on the cross.

(Col 1:15–20)

In this passage, Paul begins by asserting the universality of Christ's *creative* work and concludes by declaring the universality of Christ's *redemptive* work. It is through Jesus the Son of God that all things were made, and it is through him that all things are reconciled to God (see also 2 Cor 5:19). Paul's clarification that this applies to everything, "whether things on earth or things in heaven" seems to rule out any qualifying distinctions that might be made to avoid the universalist inference. Commentator David Hay notes that while verse 20 "does not explicitly promise universal salvation, it does suggest that ultimately no one will be left out." He adds that "the universalistic hope set forth in 1:20 is never rescinded, and it supports the letter's general tone of confidence and its various declarations that what God revealed and accomplished through Jesus concerns everyone and every aspect of life."[25]

Critics push back in a variety of ways, however, such as by broadening our understanding of Paul's sense of what it means for God to reconcile himself to creation. For instance, Scot McKnight says, "reconciliation encompasses the fullness of God's triumph over evil in judgment, subjugation of powers, and redemption for the saints."[26] Others interpret Paul's words to indicate a divine *aim* or *desire* to reconcile all things to himself, even if this is not ultimately achieved in the end.[27] Thus, Howard Marshall insists that the universal reconciliation to which Paul refers is of a conditional sort, where the offer of forgiveness extends to all but the actualization of this potential universal redemption depends on the faith response of each individual.[28] Finally, rather than offering an alternative interpretation of the passage, others (e.g., N. T. Wright and Scot McKnight) prefer just to insist that Paul cannot be endorsing universalism here because he so clearly teaches lim-

---

25. Hay, *Colossians*, 66.

26. McKnight, *Colossians*, 166. Similarly, Douglas Moo interprets such reconciliation as encompassing God's enabling his covenant people "to live in a dangerous and hostile world in peace" and bringing "his entire rebellious creation back under the rule of his sovereign power" (*Colossians and Philemon*, 137).

27. See, for example, Barclay, *Philippians, Colossians, and Thessalonians*, 124.

28. Marshall, "New Testament," 17–30.

ited salvation in his other writings. The trouble for non-universalists, of course, is that Paul appears to teach universalism in some other texts too.

The Two Adams: 1 Corinthians 15:22 and Romans 5:12–19

Such passages appear in two places where Paul draws a parallel between the first and second Adam. In 1 Corinthians 15, he writes, "as in Adam all die, so in Christ all will be made alive" (v. 22), and a little later Paul notes that as a consequence of Christ's redeeming work, he will have complete dominion so that "God may be all in all" (v. 28). Paul draws out this parallel between Adam and Jesus much more extensively in Romans 5. There he writes, "sin entered the world through one man, and death through sin, and in this way death came to all people, because all sinned" (v. 12). A few verses later, he notes that

> the gift is not like the trespass. For if the many died by the trespass of the one man, how much more did God's grace and the gift that came by the grace of the one man, Jesus Christ, overflow to the many! Nor can the gift of God be compared with the result of one man's sin: The judgment followed one sin and brought condemnation, but the gift followed many trespasses and brought justification. For if, by the trespass of the one man, death reigned through that one man, how much more will those who receive God's abundant provision of grace and of the gift of righteousness reign in life through the one man, Jesus Christ! Consequently, just as one trespass resulted in condemnation for all people, so also one righteous act resulted in justification and life for all people. For just as through the disobedience of the one man the many were made sinners, so also through the obedience of the one man the many will be made righteous.
>
> (Rom 5:15–19)

A common universalist inference here is that since original sin was passed on to all human beings through the sin of a representative federal head, Adam, in parallel fashion, the righteousness of God will be passed on to all human beings through the perfect life of our representative federal head, Jesus Christ, who is the second Adam. Regarding the Romans 5 passage, Robin Parry comments,

> What is of special note . . . is the universal results of both the disobedience of Adam and the obedience of Christ. Adam's sin

brought condemnation and death to *all* people (compare 3:23). Christ's righteous act brings justification and eternal life to *all* people. Indeed, Paul is at pains to make clear that the "all people" who were "made sinners" and "condemned" are the *very same* "all people" who will be "made righteous" and who, in Christ, are justified and have life.²⁹

So Parry, like Thomas Talbott among others, regards this passage as explicitly teaching universalism.³⁰

There are several non-universalist interpretations of these Romans 5 and 1 Corinthians 15 passages. We will focus on the former since it is the more detailed and substantive text. One approach is to say that the meaning of "all" and "many" in each case should be restricted to those who are *in* Adam and *in* Christ, respectively. In the former case, this would naturally include everyone, since all human beings are descended from Adam and thus born in sin. And in the latter case, all who are in Christ will be justified and receive eternal life, but of course this does not mean that all are actually in Christ. Thus, for example, Craig Keener says, "'the many' in this context refers to all who are defined by their relationship to either Adam or Christ."³¹ Closely related to this approach is perhaps the most common non-universalist take on this passage, which is to insist that Paul's use of "all" refers to those to whom salvation is *offered* rather than those who re-

---

29. MacDonald (Parry), *Evangelical Universalist*, 79–80. It is worth noting that the parallels Parry highlights here break down somewhat on an Arminian perspective, because on this view the justification of sinners through Christ's work is contingent upon the free-will response of sinners, whereas the universality of original sin is independent and prior to particular choices of the descendants of Adam. In contrast, this universalist argument by analogy appears more compelling within a Calvinist theological framework, where both the divine decree of the curse of original sin and the divine decree of the justification of all people (on the universalist view) are independent of particular human wills. And all human choices, whether to rebel because of original sin or to repent and choose Christ because of divine election, are alike the *consequences* of universal divine decree. So it would appear that a Calvinist doctrine of election maximizes the force of the universalist's analogical argument. And given the universalist conviction that all will be saved, the most significant concerns about the Calvinist doctrine of predestination—specifically, regarding the problem of evil—should be assuaged anyway. After all, if everyone is saved in the end, then all divinely ordained suffering and rebellion are merely temporary and, arguably, for the long-term benefit of all.

30. Käsemann goes so far as to say that regarding the Pauline literature generally, "all powerful grace is unthinkable without eschatological universalism" (*Romans*, 157).

31. Keener, *Romans*, 77. Another scholar who takes such an approach is Hodge, *Romans*, 269.

ceive this offer and are actually saved.[32] Other commentators focus on the intention of "all" and "many" in these passages and read these terms as referring to all or many *kinds* of people, including both Jews and gentiles and believers both past and future. Thus, Paul's point is to note that both the sin of Adam and justification in Christ apply to "all without distinction," rather than to "all without exception."[33]

Universalists typically counter these approaches by insisting that such interpretations are an imposition on the text, since there is nothing in these passages to recommend such a delimitation of the meaning of "all," whether in Romans 5:18 or 1 Corinthians 15:22. Some commentators concede that these passages do appear to affirm universalism but that this cannot be the all-things-considered Pauline position, since his writings elsewhere affirm a particularist position on human salvation.[34] This is not a popular non-universalist interpretive stance, however, since it attributes a certain incoherence to Paul's thinking on the subject, though those sympathetic with this approach might more charitably regard it as simply a "tension" in his thought.

Every Knee Shall Bow: Philippians 2:9–11 and Romans 10:9–13

Another universalist argument emerges from the conjunction of two more Pauline texts that together create a syllogism apparently pointing to the salvation of all humanity. One of these appears in the Philippians 2 *kenosis* passage: "Therefore God exalted him to the highest place and gave him the name that is above every name, that at the name of Jesus every knee should bow, in heaven and on earth and under the earth, and every tongue acknowledge that Jesus Christ is Lord, to the glory of God the Father" (Phil 2:9–11). Notice Paul's concern to clarify the universality of this confession of Christ. The natural question, then, is whether such confession of Christ is always effectual for salvation. Another Pauline passage would suggest that it is:

---

32. See, for example, Cranfield, *Romans*, 121–22; Morris, *Romans*, 240; Schreiner, *Romans*, 291–92; Stott, *Romans*, 159; Witherington III, *Paul's Letter*, 150–51.

33. This approach is taken by Jewett, *Romans*, 385–86.

34. See Boring, "Language," 269–92 and de Boer, *Defeat of Death*, 173–75.

Hell and Divine Goodness

> If you declare with your mouth, "Jesus is Lord," and believe in your heart that God raised him from the dead, you will be saved. For it is with your heart that you believe and are justified, and it is with your mouth that you profess your faith and are saved. As Scripture says, "Anyone who believes in him will never be put to shame." For there is no difference between Jew and gentile—the same Lord is Lord of all and richly blesses all who call on him, for, "Everyone who calls on the name of the Lord will be saved."
>
> (Rom 10:9–13)

In this passage Paul applies no qualification that such calling upon the Lord must be done during one's earthly life. Thus, universalists sometimes claim that, in light of the Philippians 2 promise that all will eventually confess Christ, this constitutes strong biblical evidence for their view.[35]

In response, non-universalists have argued that the sort of confession Paul has in mind in the Romans 10 passage is that of sincere belief and saving repentance, but at the eschaton some will confess Christ only out of sorrowful regret or forced submission, which will not be effectual unto salvation. Peter O'Brien writes, "although all things will *finally* unite to bow in the name of Jesus and to acknowledge him as Lord . . . it is not to be assumed that this will be done gladly by all."[36] And Millard Erickson adds, "we must picture the wicked not as eagerly joining forces with the Lord, but as surrendering to a conquering army, so to speak. There will be an acquiescence in defeat, not a joyful commitment."[37] But does such a concept of unwilling subjection to Christ really work for the non-universalist? Thomas Talbott suggests that this approach is actually incoherent, since "if the powers and principalities of which Paul speaks are *competing wills*, then as a matter of logic these powers and principalities could never be *entirely* in subjection to Christ against their will; for if they should be subjugated against their will, then their *will* would precisely not be in subjection to Christ."[38] In any case, it appears that the force of this argument from Philippians 2 and Romans 10 will depend upon one's view of the possibility of post-mortem conversion, which is something regarding which the Scriptures are largely silent.

---

35. Yale University philosopher Keith DeRose makes this argument in his "Universalism and the Bible: The Really Good News": http://campuspress.yale.edu/keithderose/1129-2/#7. See also MacDonald (Parry), *Evangelical Universalist*, 97–100.

36. O'Brien, *Colossians and Philemon*, 56.

37. Erickson, *Christian Theology*, 1236.

38. Talbott, *Inescapable*, 68.

The Appeal to Divine Desire and Unlimited Atonement

A final argument for universalism reasons that we can be confident that all will be saved simply because God himself desires universal salvation and God is able to accomplish whatever he desires. That God wants everyone to be saved seems clear from 2 Peter 3:9, which says God does "not wan[t] anyone to perish, but everyone to come to repentance." Paul says, "God has bound everyone over to disobedience so that he may have mercy on them all" (Rom 11:32) and God "wants all people to be saved and to come to a knowledge of the truth" (1 Tim 2:4). Also, divine intention to save everyone appears evident in recurrent biblical assertions that Christ died for the entire world. Jesus Christ "takes away the sin of the world" (John 1:29). He died for all (2 Cor 5:14–15); he tasted death for everyone (Heb 2:9); he "gave himself as a ransom for all people" (1 Tim 2:6); and Christ "is the atoning sacrifice for our sins, and not only for ours but also for the sins of the whole world" (1 John 2:2). This last passage is especially noteworthy since John seems careful to emphasize that the atonement of Christ is not limited to particular groups of people but really applies to every human being, believing and unbelieving alike. Despite this, non-universalists typically insist that the intention of the passage is that the atoning work of Christ is *available* to everyone but *efficacious* only for the elect. As John Stott puts it, "a universal pardon is offered for (the sins of) the whole world and is enjoyed by those who embrace it."[39] In support of this critical distinction, commentators usually appeal to the claim that it is the only way to avoid the conclusion that John contradicts himself in the same letter, since he seems to affirm particular redemption in such passages as 1 John 1:5–10, 2:28, 3:14–15, and 5:12,16.

Some Problems for Universalism

Whatever force there might be in the above arguments for universalism, there remain some especially serious difficulties for the view. One of these regards the matter of the unforgivable sin. Jesus says, "every kind of sin and slander can be forgiven, but blasphemy against the Spirit will not be forgiven. Anyone who speaks a word against the Son of Man will be forgiven, but anyone who speaks against the Holy Spirit will not be forgiven, either

---

39. Stott, *Letters of John*, 89. Or, as Daniel L. Akin puts it, "universal in *provision* is not to be equated with universal in *application*" (*1, 2, 3 John*, 84).

in this age or in the age to come" (Matt 12:31–32). How can the universalist get around what seems to be the direct implication of this passage that some will not be saved? (This assumes, of course, that some people are actually guilty of the unforgivable sin, which seems to be a safe assumption given that Jesus bothers to mention it.) One recourse available to the universalist is to appeal to the idea that "unforgivable" might simply mean that if you commit such a sin, then you must be punished for it. But this doesn't necessarily mean that you cannot fully pay for it and then be set free and finally reconciled to God.[40] Consider a thief who is convicted and sentenced for his crime, serves his time and is finally set free and "reconciled" to society. The thief was never forgiven but paid his own debt in full. Perhaps the situation with the unforgivable sin is analogous. That is a sin for which the blood of Christ will never atone, but the guilty sinner must take the punishment for it himself. Yet, perhaps full reconciliation with God may be possible after that punishment has been meted out.

Another problem for universalism concerns the doctrine of the elect—the special chosen people of God emphasized in the Pauline literature (Rom 9:11; 11:7, 28; 2 Tim 2:10; Titus 1:1), as well as by Jesus (Matt 24:22–31; Mark 13:20–27) and Peter (1 Pet 1:1; 2 Pet 1:10). If all people are ultimately saved, then everyone is actually among the elect, so then of what use is the distinction? There are at least two potentially helpful routes of response available to the universalist. One approach would be to argue that the elect/non-elect distinction is only temporary, applicable during our earthly sojourn but not in the eschaton.[41] Another approach would be to grant that the category of the elect is indeed permanent, but it is not a soteriological distinction. Rather, for example, it might be a category which distinguishes certain people *positionally*, whether in terms of their ministerial function on earth and/or their status or role in the afterlife.

Finally, there is the problem of the "everlasting destruction" of the wicked referenced in 2 Thessalonians 1:9. If a person is ultimately saved and reconciled to God, then how can her punishment be said to be "everlasting"? Parry deals with this by proposing that the word which is typically translated as "destruction" in 2 Thessalonians 1:9 (*olethron*) can also be

---

40. As universalist George MacDonald says, "if sin demands punishment, and the righteous punishment is given, then the man is free" ("Justice," 349).

41. Sven Hillert deploys this strategy in his *Limited and Universal Salvation*. See especially pp. 144–48.

rendered as "ruin," which need not be regarded as a permanent condition.[42] Other universalists, such as Thomas Talbott, grant that the text may be read as asserting permanent destruction but propose that this destruction concerns the annihilation of the person's *sinful nature* not the annihilation of the person herself.[43] A difficulty with this approach is that after noting that the wicked are destined for "everlasting destruction" Paul adds that they will be "shut out from the presence of the Lord and from the glory of his might on the day [Christ] comes to be glorified in his holy people and to be marveled at among all those who have believed" (2 Thess. 1:9–10). Such exclusion seems to regard the entire person, not solely her sinful nature. However, Thomas Talbott challenges the NIV translation of this text, insisting that what is actually "from the presence of the Lord," according to Paul, is not the sinner ([shut out] from the presence) but the punishment ([which comes] from the presence). Thus, they suffer "eternal punishment, which is from the presence of the Lord." But even if one goes with Talbott's alternative translation, the object of the destruction is still *the wicked people themselves*, not just an aspect of them (i.e., their sinful nature).

CONCLUSION

We have now reviewed many of the biblical arguments for and against each of the three perspectives on hell. Hopefully, it is clear that each view enjoys at least some *prima facie* biblical support. On the traditionalist side, the strongest evidence derives from the two passages from Revelation that seem to affirm that the devil, beast, and false prophet suffer forever in the lake of fire. However, the fact that neither of these passages affirms that humans suffer a similar fate means that the support for the traditional doctrine of hell is only indirect. Furthermore, when building a case for one's view on the literal truth about hell—or any other doctrine for that matter—to ground that doctrine primarily upon two passages from a highly figurative, apocalyptic text is problematic. As for universalism, given that this view has been affirmed by a small minority of Christians for most of church history, the case for this view might appear surprisingly strong. It is certainly the most hopeful. What mercifully minded lover of reconciliation wouldn't want everyone to be saved in the end? But the biblical teachings of unforgivable sin, the doctrine of the elect, and the "everlasting destruction"

---

42. See MacDonald (Parry), *Evangelical Universalist*, 152.
43. Talbott, *Inescapable*, 92–98.

and even the vanishing memory of the damned present serious problems for this view. As for conditionalism, the strong biblical themes of the destruction of the wicked and the opposition of death and eternal life point toward the ultimate annihilation of the damned. These themes, combined with the lack of definitive biblical support for eternal conscious torment and some significant textual challenges for universalism, give me the sense that, from an exegetical standpoint, conditionalism has the most scriptural support among the three views. But whatever perspective one affirms on the issue, when it comes to the biblical testimony, it is clear that each view enjoys some evidential warrant, while each also has its problems. This accounts for the indecisiveness of the early church as well as the continuing debate about the issue throughout the rest of church history. Perhaps we should follow the counsel of theologian David Lotz and adopt an attitude of "reverent agnosticism" when it comes to the biblical data regarding personal eschatology.[44] In any case, the lack of scriptural conclusiveness reinforces the need for close philosophical analysis of the doctrine of hell in order to tilt the evidential balance in a particular direction. The remainder of this book is devoted to just such philosophical inquiry.

---

44. Lotz, "Heaven and Hell," 90.

2

Hell and Divine Justice

In the previous chapter we reviewed major biblical arguments for and against the three standard views of hell. We found that the biblical witness is not entirely conclusive in favor of any of these three views, which strongly reinforces the need for a philosophical inquiry into the issue to see what additional insight this might provide. This chapter commences that inquiry with a close look into a philosophical concept that is central to the whole debate: justice. If we begin with the assumption that God is perfectly just in the sense that he is fair in his dealings with people, then we may assess the doctrine of hell accordingly. That is, we may ask of each of the three views whether the fate of the damned they affirm is ultimately fair. What does it mean to be morally fair or just in one's treatment of others? Minimally, it seems, to be just is to treat people equitably in the sense of applying a common moral standard to all without regard to morally irrelevant considerations. Since such fairness or justice seems to be a basic moral good and since God is perfectly good, we are warranted in expecting that God will always treat people equitably, applying the same moral standard to all and never causing anyone unwarranted or disproportionate harm.[1]

---

1. While I affirm that God is perfectly just and fair in his dealings with human beings, this is not to say that God has obligations towards us. I am sympathetic with the thought of many Christian thinkers, from Anselm to Marilyn McCord Adams, that God is not obligated to human beings and, correlatively, humans have no rights to claim against God. On this point, Adams writes, "created persons have *no rights* against God, because God has *no obligations* to creatures: in particular, God has no obligation to be good to us; no obligation not to ruin us whether by depriving our lives of positive meaning, by

Hell and Divine Goodness

When it comes to the doctrine of hell, the question of justice arises on a number of fronts. We may begin with the very idea of post-mortem punishment. Is it just to apply punitive consequences that extend beyond a person's earthly life, despite the fact that all of their sins were committed on earth? And, as regards traditionalism and conditionalism, is it just that these consequences should be permanent in effect when the performance of the deeds that warranted these consequences was transitory? Regarding the first question, post-mortem punishment not only seems appropriate from a justice standpoint but necessary, given that perfect justice cannot be achieved in this world. Furthermore, as Thomas Oden notes, "if the consequences of sin extend beyond one's finite life, then it is not morally scandalous for the punishment of sin also to extend beyond one's finite life."[2] As to the permanency of consequences for temporary acts on earth, this is a far more difficult matter which takes us to some of the core issues under consideration in this book.[3]

Traditionalists maintain that the damned suffer everlasting torment, and typically they claim that such perpetual suffering is warranted as a form of retributive punishment. Some traditionalists, however, prefer to see hell more as a natural consequence of vicious living and rejection of God. In either case, we may inquire as to the justice of eternal conscious torment (ECT) as a retributively punitive or negatively consequential outcome for the damned. Similarly for conditionalists, hell may be seen in terms of retributive justice or the natural consequence of a wicked life or turning from God. On this view, although punishment in hell may be of very long duration, it eventually culminates in complete annihilation, thus bringing an end to conscious torment, though, arguably, not an end to the punishment, since the person annihilated remains extinct forever. Here, too, we may ask, is this a just outcome for some persons? And, finally, we must ask the same question of universalism. Are hell's sufferings warranted to the extent that

---

producing or allowing the deterioration or disintegration of our personalities, by destroying our bodies, or by annihilating us" ("Problem of Hell," 324; emphases in original).

2. Oden, *Life in the Spirit*, 456.

3. Aquinas says, "the fact that adultery or murder is committed in a moment does not call for a momentary punishment" (*Summa Theologica*, 975). This is an analogy that proponents of all three views can accept, in so far as it prompts us to affirm the justice of a long-lasting post-mortem penalty for earthly sins. However, traditionalists and conditionalists disagree with universalists over whether that consequence is everlasting. And traditionalists and conditionalists disagree over the *nature* of that everlasting consequence.

they are experienced by people in hell, albeit to a limited degree and though ultimately followed by eternal bliss? Naturally, this question is not nearly as pressing for the universalist as it is for advocates of the other views, because the ending is always a happy one, and, as Shakespeare has said, all's well that ends well. But the question regarding restorationism still warrants consideration, since all human suffering is a morally serious matter.

A major source of disagreement among proponents of traditionalism and conditionalism regards the *proportionality criterion*, according to which the severity of a punishment must match the severity of the offense. Otherwise, the punishment would cause undue harm and therefore be unjust. Some traditionalists and conditionalists—in particular, those who share a retributivist view of punishment—disagree over which form of punishment is properly proportioned to human guilt and, therefore, fits best with belief in a perfectly just God. Conditionalists have often argued that ECT is problematic because unending torment is too severe, given that the sins of any human being are finite. Traditionalists, however, insist that ECT is warranted either because the perfect moral status of the one sinned against, namely God, requires infinite punishment or because the damned perpetually sin in hell, thus deserving perpetual punishment. Significantly, the discussion has usually proceeded on the assumption that ECT is a more extreme punishment than annihilation (even if the latter follows some period of conscious torment). This assumption itself warrants critical review. In this chapter all of these issues will be discussed in detail.

THE JUSTICE ARGUMENT AGAINST ETERNAL CONSCIOUS TORMENT AND SOME LINES OF RESPONSE

Let us begin by considering the justice of hell on the traditional view. By far, among accounts of hell, it is the doctrine of eternal conscious torment that has been most vigorously critiqued throughout Christian history. Regarding the casting of sinners into hell for eternity, David Lewis declares, "what God does is . . . infinitely worse than what the worst of tyrants did," because "the punishment of the damned is infinitely disproportionate to their crimes."[4] This is variously called the "justice argument" or "disproportionality argument" against ECT, and it goes roughly as follows. Given

---

4. Lewis, "Divine Evil," 472.

a retributivist perspective, the punishment for any offense should fit the transgression in terms of severity. Eternal conscious torment *far exceeds* what is punitively appropriate for finite sins, however wicked a person's conduct might have been during her earthly sojourn. So ECT in hell is unjust in any case. Since God is perfectly just we can be confident that he would never punish in this way. Therefore, the traditional view must be false.

The misgiving expressed above by Lewis, and shared by many conditionalists and universalists, regarding ECT concerns a basic disproportionality. In a context of retribution, justice entails a due proportion of degree of punishment to the offense. But being everlasting in duration, ECT appears to fail this standard in the extreme. How have traditionalists met this criticism? St. Augustine, the greatest early church proponent of ECT, conceded that infinite punishment does *appear* excessive, but he accounted for this in terms of the limits of human reason: "Eternal punishment seems hard and unjust to human perceptions, because in the weakness of our mortal condition there is wanting that highest and purest wisdom by which it can be perceived how great a wickedness was committed in that first transgression."[5] But, of course, even granting that we all lack the wisdom of God to fully comprehend the depth of human wickedness, there must be some rational grounds for ECT. What could possibly justify endless suffering in hell? It appears that the possible grounds for such a justification are either that the *character* or the *acts* of the condemned person are infinitely wicked. Most traditionalists affirm some version of the latter approach, and these are distinguished based on whether the infinite wickedness of the acts of the condemned is due to the *nature* of their sinful actions (i.e., whom they offend) or the *number* of their sinful actions. So, as we will see, this suggests three possible routes for the traditionalist to defend ECT, specifically by appealing to (1) the character of the offender, (2) the nature of the person offended (in this case, God), or (3) the perpetual sinful acts of the offender in hell. We will consider each of these in turn.

Appeal to the Character of the Offender

The basic claim of the character-based punishment approach to justifying ECT is that fallen human beings are infinitely vicious and thus deserve to suffer in hell for all eternity. There is some initial plausibility to this approach

---

5. Augustine, *City of God*, 706.

because (1) arguably, all moral desert reduces to considerations of personal character and (2) all human beings are guilty by virtue of original sin, the innate corruption of all persons due to their being descended from Adam. As to the idea that all moral desert ultimately pertains to character, some argue that this follows from the fact that all of a person's acts, motives, attitudes, and dispositions either *constitute* or *flow from* their character.[6] So moral desert based on any of these particular aspects of a person will pertain to features of their moral character or natural products of their character. In either case, a person's character is the proper substrate of moral assessment. Now since Scripture teaches, and the Christian theological tradition has affirmed as essential to orthodoxy, that all human moral characters are fundamentally morally corrupt, the default human moral standing before God is that of deserving severe punishment. But is human moral character *infinitely* vicious such that ECT could be a just punishment for unredeemed people?

First, let us consider what it would even *mean* to say that a person's character is infinitely wicked. One might mean by this that a person has an infinite *number* of bad motives or attitudes, but this seems impossible given human mental limits, at least during our lives on earth. Alternatively, we might prefer to think of a person's vicious motives and attitudes as being infinitely *intense*. But finite human mental capacity seems to rule this out as well.[7] A further problem is the fact that morally good motives and attitudes in human beings are finite capacities. Motives to love and help others and dispositions to be kind, courageous, generous, and patient arguably have upper limits. If these morally virtuous character traits have upper limits, then it would appear that those traits at the other end of the moral spectrum, vices, would likewise have upper limits or a maximum wickedness quotient. So we wouldn't normally say that a person is infinitely virtuous; rather we should say they are *perfectly* virtuous—as in the case of Jesus Christ. Similarly, it seems odd to say that someone, even Satan himself, is infinitely vicious; rather we should say that he is *maximally* vicious. And if wickedness has an upper limit, then it's a mistake to appeal to infinite wickedness as grounds for an infinitely severe punishment in the form of ECT.

A further problem with the character-based punishment approach to justifying ECT regards human freedom. A widely shared moral intuition

---

6. Stephen Kershnar uses this argument in defense of character-based punishment in his "Hell and Punishment," 124.

7. I have borrowed this argument from Kershnar's "Hell and Punishment," 125.

is that moral desert is based at least in part on what we *do*—our actions, words, and thoughts, not just our character or dispositions to act in particular ways. In support of this, it is generally agreed that our moral character is, at least in part, the result of free conscious choices that we make. So it would stand to reason that moral desert tracks on actions as well as or perhaps instead of character.

A third problem with the character-based punishment approach pertains to an implication of this view when conjoined with the doctrine of original sin.[8] If all human beings are infinitely vicious due to their corrupt characters and this is due to original sin and thus innately true of every person, then it follows that even infants and toddlers, perhaps even fetuses, are as guilty before God as any adult human being. It follows from this that no matter how viciously a person lives throughout an entire lifetime of, say, eighty years, he or she is no more deserving of ECT than a newborn baby or perhaps even a first-trimester fetus. This implication problematically diminishes the significance of the moral life—the importance of living virtuously and fulfilling our duties to one another. For if even utter moral failure throughout my life means I'm no more vicious than a newborn baby, then why bother to be virtuous? Furthermore, it implies that God would be perfectly just in sentencing the soul of a stillborn baby or aborted fetus to suffer eternally in hell, even without that person's making a single voluntary choice in their lifetime.[9] But this severely violates the proportionality criterion. Whatever ideas about divine justice we might entertain, whether *a priori* or biblically based, the prospect of God subjecting someone to eternal conscious torment without their ever having committed a single sin,

---

8. In affirming the doctrine of original sin, Augustine wrote, "the whole human race was condemned in its apostate head by a divine judgment so just that even if not a single member of the race were ever saved from it, no one could rail against God's justice" (*Confessions and Enchiridion*, 99). Similarly, John Calvin declared that "whether a man is a guilty unbeliever or an innocent believer, he begets not innocent but guilty children, for he begets them from a corrupted nature" (*Institutes*, 250).

9. About this implication, George MacDonald writes, "the notion that a creature born imperfect, nay, born with impulses to evil not of his own generating, and which he could not help having, a creature to whom the true face of God was never presented, and by whom it never could have been seen, should be thus condemned, is as loathsome a lie against God as could find a place in a heart too undeveloped to understand what justice is, and too low to look up into the face of Jesus. It never in truth found place in any heart, though in many a pettifogging brain. There is but one thing lower than deliberately to believe such a lie, and that is to worship the God of whom it is believed" ("Justice," 352).

whether in act, word, or deed, is difficult to square with the concept of God being truly just, much less loving and kind.

Appeal to the Nature of God: The Status Argument

Historically, many Christian theologians and philosophers have defended the justice of ECT based on who it is that all human sins ultimately offend, namely God. Such traditionalists argue that the degree of severity of any offense must be understood in terms of the nature of the one offended. Since God is infinitely good, any sin against him is infinitely heinous. For this reason, even a single sin, however seemingly minute, deserves infinite punishment. This mode of thinking about the matter has a long history. For example, Aquinas reasons that sin "is the turning away from the immutable good, which is infinite, wherefore, in this respect, sin is infinite.... Accordingly, in so far as sin consists in turning away from something, its corresponding punishment is the *pain of loss*, which also is infinite, because it is the loss of the infinite good, i.e., God."[10] And Jonathan Edwards articulates the argument this way:

> Our obligation to love, honor, and obey any being, is in proportion to his loveliness, honorableness, and authority.... But God is a being infinitely lovely.... He is a being of infinite greatness, majesty, and glory; and therefore is infinitely honorable.... His authority over us is infinite; and the ground of his right to our obedience, is infinitely strong.... So that sin against God being a violation of infinite obligations, must be a crime infinitely heinous; and so deserving of infinite punishment.[11]

So Edwards concludes, "If there be any evil or faultiness in sin against God, there is certainly infinite evil: for if it be any fault at all, it has an infinite aggravation, viz. that it is against an infinite object."[12] These theological luminaries and many contemporary traditionalists agree that, because of the greatness of God and our concomitant duties toward him, all sin is infinitely evil and thus warrants an infinite punishment. The underlying principle to which their arguments appeal is what is sometimes called the "status principle," which is the idea that the degree of an offender's guilt

---

10. Aquinas, *Summa Theologica*, 975–76.
11. Edwards, "Justice of God," 342–43.
12. Ibid., 343.

is always proportionate to the status of the offended person.[13] Let us call the argument in defense of ECT based on this principle (such as those by Aquinas and Edwards noted above) the "status argument." Conditionalists usually resist the status argument[14] because they assume that to concede it adds considerable philosophical force to the doctrine of ECT. But is this really so? Not if annihilation is at least as severe a punishment as ECT. There are, I believe, several reasons for thinking that annihilation is even more severe than ECT. But because this is a lengthy debate that I want to pursue in detail, I will put this off until later in the chapter.

For now, let us consider the reasonableness of the status argument and the status principle upon which it is founded. The first thing worth noting is that those who affirm the status principle fail to adequately defend it. It is simply assumed by many traditionalists that the infinite greatness of God implies the infinite guilt of anyone who offends God. And those who do bother to defend this claim often do so with flimsy analogies, such as one mentioned by Aquinas, which appeals to the fact that to harm a national leader is more grievous than harming a private citizen.[15] While this is true, analogies that point in a different direction are just as easy to come by. For example, Marilyn Adams offers this thought experiment:

> Suppose that Schweitzer and Gandhi are equally saintly and that Green and White are equally unsavory characters with long criminal records. Suppose that on separate occasions Green gratuitously slaps Schweitzer in the face, Schweitzer gratuitously slaps White in the face, and Gandhi gratuitously slaps Schweitzer in the face. If guilt were proportional, not just to the offence, but to the moral uprightness of the offended party, then Green would incur more guilt and liability to punishment than would Schweitzer. For since Schweitzer is worthier than White, Green's failure to show respect for Schweitzer was more grievous than Schweitzer's failure to show respect for White. Similarly, Gandhi's action would be more culpable than Schweitzer's. In fact, I think we are more apt to consider guilt as directly proportional to the nature of the offender than to the nature of the offended party. Schweitzer's action in slapping White is, if anything, more culpable than Green's action in

---

13. For contemporary defenses of the status principle, see Crisp, "Divine Retribution," 39–44; Paul Kabay, "status principle," 91–103; and Bawulski, "Annihilationism," 73–75.

14. Universalists have been critical as well. See Adams, "God of Justice," 441–44 and Talbott, "Punishment, Forgiveness, and Divine Justice," 151–68.

15. Aquinas, *Summa Theologica*, 975.

slapping Schweitzer. In view of Schweitzer's long-standing habits of self-control and moral behavior, we should expect more from him than from Green who has never developed those habits.[16]

Adams' analysis here seems on the mark. At least in the sort of situation she describes, degree of guilt does hinge more on the nature of the offender than that of the offended party. So while Aquinas' illustration might establish grounds for accepting a nature-of-the-offended standard in some moral-offense contexts, Adams' illustration establishes grounds for a nature-of-the-offender standard in other contexts. So which of these ought we to use when it comes to the moral-offense context of sins against God? Based on thought experiments alone, the question seems undecidable. And since it is the traditionalist who is making the strong claim in support of the status principle, the burden of proof remains on her to demonstrate its truth, even in the absence of counter-arguments.

But now consider two counter-arguments that make it even more problematic to accept the status principle. Presumably, God's great moral status is a matter of virtue, as is the case of any morally laudable being. If, as noted earlier, virtues have upper limits, then this is true of God as well. To say that God is morally perfect is just to say that God is maximally virtuous in every category—perfectly generous, perfectly kind, perfectly patient, etc. But to say God is maximally virtuous is not to say he is infinitely virtuous.[17] So if the degree of guilt in any offense against God is properly determined by God's moral status, then it follows that human guilt is at most *maximally* great, not *infinitely* great. In other words, through our sin we may plummet to the greatest possible degree of guilt, but that is not infinite guilt. This might sound like small consolation on Judgment Day, but the difference is, well, infinite. For maximal guilt, as great as that is, is still finite in terms of severity. And finite guilt, however great, presumably does not warrant endless punishment in the form of ECT.

Secondly, the status principle has absurd implications. If a single sin implies infinite guilt before God, then upon committing my first sin as a small child I became infinitely wicked and guilty before God. This undermines all moral distinctions between people. Common sense tells us that people are more or less morally virtuous and that across the human

---

16. Adams, "God of Justice," 443.

17. God's virtuous traits might have endless ongoing applications, but this would not imply that at any time in history God would have completed an actually infinite number of virtuous acts.

Hell and Divine Goodness

population there is a broad moral spectrum, from extremely wicked to extremely virtuous people. But if the status principle is true, then since all have sinned we are all *equally* wicked because we are all *infinitely* guilty before God. Given the biblical teaching that "all have sinned and fall short of the glory of God" (Rom 3:23), we must grant that all are guilty before God and in need of redemption we cannot provide for ourselves. But this is no grounds, nor is there any biblical evidence for,[18] the claim that we are all *equally* or *infinitely* guilty before God.[19]

I want to conclude this section with a consideration of an argument that demonstrates that both of the approaches to defending ECT thus far discussed are seriously problematic. Specifically, I want to point out why appeals both to the character of the offender and appeals to the nature of God, via the status principle, severely violate the proportionality criterion and thus constitute extreme and pervasive injustices.

On these two accounts of the traditional view of hell, the damned are infinitely guilty and this is why they deserve to suffer ECT. Infinite guilt warrants infinite punishment, hence the need for the damned to suffer endlessly in hell. On the face of it, this seems appropriately just, but there is actually a severe disparity here that is usually overlooked—a disparity between the moral crimes of the damned and the actual punishment they receive, given the assumptions of traditionalism thus far discussed. If the damned truly are guilty of infinite sin and thus deserve infinite torment, then they can never be justly punished. For at any given moment in their career in hell, no matter how many millions of years of torment they have suffered, there always remains more sin that needs to be punished. And this

---

18. Not only is there a lack of biblical evidence in favor of this idea but there is also positive biblical evidence *against* it. For example, the notion of equal and infinite human guilt is difficult to square with the biblical teaching that there are degrees of punishment in hell. In Luke 10, Jesus declares to the people of Chorazin and Bethsaida that "it will be more bearable for Tyre and Sidon at the judgment than for you" (v. 14). And elsewhere Jesus says, "The servant who knows the master's will and does not get ready or does not do what the master wants will be beaten with many blows. But the one who does not know and does things deserving punishment will be beaten with few blows" (Luke 12:47–48). Such passages appear to contradict the ideas of equal and infinite guilt as well as the notion of equal punishment. In light of this, nineteenth-century Anglican theologian Henry Constable declared regarding the traditionalist view of hell, "away then with this diabolical doctrine which shocks all our sense of justice and casts bitter contempt upon the merciful words of Christ. Is a life of endless agony, ever increasing, what Jesus meant by a *'few stripes'*"? ("Divine Justice," 206).

19. For further criticisms of the status argument, see Kvanvig, *Problem of Hell*, 29–55 and Marshall, "Divine and Human Punishment," 212–14.

is so for everyone in hell at any given moment in eternity: *there is always outstanding unpunished sin.*

Since the traditional doctrine of ECT implies that much sin remains unpunished eternally, it fails to meet the proportionality criterion and is extremely unjust. But the problem gets worse for the traditionalist, for the amount of unpunished sin that remains for all eternity is *infinite*. That this is so follows from the nature of infinity. For an infinite set, subtraction of any finite portion of this set does not diminish the original infinite totality, precisely because an actual infinity is endless. Thus, no matter how much the damned person has already suffered in hell, she still has an endless amount of time to suffer. That is, her future suffering remains infinite. This much is affirmed by the traditionalist in her insistence that the suffering of the damned must be endless. No amount of days, centuries, or millennia brings the damned the least bit closer to completing her term in hell. In "subtracting" from the total number of years in hell she is due, her remaining torment is not lessened in the least. Again, the traditionalist's justification for this is that the damned deserve this because their yet unpunished sin always remains infinite. And this means that infinite unpunished sin exists forever. This not only fails to satisfy the proportionality criterion but falls *infinitely* short of meeting this standard for just punishment. So from a justice standpoint, the traditional doctrine of ECT could not fail more miserably, at least on the two approaches to defending ECT discussed so far.

Appeal to Perpetual Vice: The Continuing-Sin Thesis

We have found that the first two approaches to the traditional view of hell (which defend ECT by appealing to wicked human character and divine moral perfection) are unsatisfactory because they both imply eternal injustice. The last alternative available to the traditionalist is to justify ECT by appealing to the notion that the damned are guilty of a potentially infinite number of sinful acts. Many traditionalists do so by affirming the *continuing-sin model* of hell. This is the notion that the active rebellion of the wicked does not cease with damnation but is ongoing in hell. Consequently, the endless continuation of their punishment is just. Charles Seymour advocates such a view and proposes that, "the damned have the freedom to sin even after death. If they choose to sin continually, it is fair that they suffer continually."[20] And C. S. Lewis's conception of hell appears

20. Seymour, "Hell, Justice, and Freedom," 78.

to be a version of the continuing-sin model, as is evident in his remarks that "the doors of hell are locked on the *inside*. I do not mean that the ghosts may not wish to come out of hell, in the vague fashion wherein an envious man 'wishes' to be happy. . . . They enjoy forever the horrible freedom they have demanded, and are therefore self-enslaved."[21]

So how does all of this post-mortem rebellion amount to a justification for hell's everlasting torments?[22] Michael Murray explains the reasoning as follows:

> No wrongs we do in this life *can* merit infinite punishment . . . [but] this does not mean that those in hell might not be rightly punished for eternity nonetheless. To see why, consider a criminal who commits a crime, is caught, and is then sentenced to twenty years in prison. While in prison, however, he continues to commit further crimes, and for these further crimes he receives additional sentencing time. The result is that while none of the crimes he commits merits a life sentence, the cumulative sentence for crimes committed before and while in prison is never exhausted. Likewise . . . those who are judged and sentenced to hell might not have a sentence which initially merits an infinite punishment. But their unchecked sinful desires continue to lead them to sin even in hell and so continue to mount penalties which are never satisfied.[23]

This rationale has the merit of avoiding reliance on the questionable notion of earthly sin requiring infinite punishment. By appealing to ongoing sin in hell, the notion of everlasting punishment can fit coherently with the idea that all of one's sins are finite in severity.[24]

21. Lewis, *Problem of Pain*, 127–28.

22. Nineteenth-century theologian Robert Dabney was another proponent of this view. Like Seymour and Lewis, he hypothesizes rather than arguing for the view, proposing that "if man continues to sin forever, he will continue to suffer forever. While he was paying off a previous debt of guilt he would contract an additional one and so be forever subject to penalty" (Dabney, *Systematic Theology*, 857).

23. Murray, "Heaven and Hell," 292–93.

24. Some versions of the continuing-sin view are not motivated by a concern to make sense of the justice of ECT so much as to *compensate* for the problem by playing up the goodness of God. For example, Eleonore Stump paradoxically suggests that the suffering of the damned is actually a *product* of God's love. She imagines that "in hell God provides for the damned a place in which they may still act and will in accordance with their nature, their second, self-chosen nature. . . . In so doing he treats the damned according to their nature and promotes their good; and because he is goodness itself, by maximizing the good of the damned, he comes as close as he can to uniting them with himself—that is to say, he loves them" ("Dante's Hell," 197). Noble as Stump's aims are here to defend

Let us call this the continuing-sin thesis (CST). What are we to make of it?[25] It might appear to be an *ad hoc* theory, since most traditionalists who appeal to the idea do so just as a way of resisting the justice argument against ECT without having to appeal to the problematic status argument for infinite guilt. Rarely is an argument provided as *independent* evidence for continuing sin in hell, whether philosophical, theological, or biblical. As in the cases of Seymour, Lewis, and Murray, the idea is simply proposed and explained as a way of making penal sense of ECT. However, some proponents do offer arguments for the idea. For example, D. A. Carson asks, "are we to imagine that the lost in hell love God with heart and soul and mind and strength, and their neighbors as themselves? If not, they are breaking the first and second commandments."[26] Notice that this rationale presupposes that the damned retain significant moral freedom, enough such that they can still genuinely choose to love or hate others. This assumption itself is questionable and in need of justification. But suppose we concede this point and grant that the damned are significantly free. Then why assume that all of the damned must always abuse this freedom? If they are truly free, then isn't it possible that they could at some point in eternity act rightly long enough to no longer require further punishment? In other words, CST creates grounds for thinking that the damned have a potential means of escape from hell. If so, then this undermines the standard traditionalist belief that ECT is *guaranteed* for all of the damned.

Richard Swinburne offers a perspective that might provide a way out for the traditionalist here. He suggests that as the damned continue to sin in hell they lock themselves into such a degenerate state that they are no longer capable of making a positive choice to extricate themselves. He explains as follows:

> We may describe a man in this situation of having lost his capacity to overrule his desires as having "lost his soul." Such a man is a prisoner of bad desires. He can no longer choose to resist them by doing the action which he judges to be overall the best thing to do. He has no natural desires to do the actions of heaven and he

---

the traditional view of hell against certain criticisms, it leaves the bulk of those addressed in this chapter untouched.

25. For an excellent analysis of the argument and its limits when considered in light of a variety of conceptions of the traditional view of hell, see Himma, "Eternally Incorrigible," 61–78.

26. Carson, *Gagging of God*, 534.

cannot choose to do them because he sees them to be of supreme worth. There is no "he" left to make that choice.[27]

This is an interesting idea and, for all I know, it might be an accurate description of the damned, if only temporarily. Unfortunately for the traditionalist, this theory takes with one hand as it gives with the other. For although it relieves the traditionalist of the escape problem related to CST, it also reintroduces the original problem, which is that of making sense of perpetually punishable sin and guilt in the damned. To wit, it's hard to see how there could be any more sin and consequent guilt emerging from them when there remains no basis for any kind of moral agency. If, as Swinburne puts it, there is no "he" left at this stage of damnation, then "he" is no longer really *free* to make good choices. And where there is no moral freedom, there can be no continuing sin.

Proponents of CST might have good responses to these issues I raise. Perhaps this approach is neither *ad hoc* nor really susceptible to the escape problem. But there are other problems far more serious, even devastating to the continuing-sin thesis. First, there is a problem with the very idea of continuing sin. For, on this view, moral evil—the continuing sin of the damned—remains eternally and so the damned in hell are never ultimately justly punished. This is because, *ex hypothesi*, the sins of those in hell never stop, so the proportionality criterion can never be fully met. It is curious that a problem so obvious should be overlooked by proponents of the view. Moreover, in appealing to this idea to solve the problem of unjust disproportionality in ECT, they not only fail to account for final justice but create another problem just as big—eternally lingering moral evil. We will discuss this problem in more detail in the next chapter.

So it appears that CST is not a significant improvement on the other two views. For all three accounts fail to meet the proportionality criterion and thus imply a state of extreme injustice for the damned. There is one aspect of CST, however, that admittedly qualifies it as a small advance from the other approaches to defending ECT. This is the fact that on CST unpunished sin is not *itself* infinite, as on the other views. Rather, on CST, sin is everlastingly real but as a potential infinite rather than an actual infinite. This, of course, is little consolation for the traditionalist given that eternal injustice, even in this finite sense, is such a serious problem.

---

27. Swinburne, "Theodicy," 49.

IS ANNIHILATION A MORE SEVERE PUNISHMENT THAN ETERNAL CONSCIOUS TORMENT?

In our earlier discussion of the status argument for ECT, we noted that traditionalists and conditionalists usually agree that ECT is a more severe punishment than annihilation of the damned. Indeed, this is the key assumption driving the traditionalist's affirmation of ECT. Since the damned are infinitely guilty, they deserve the most severe punishment possible— namely, ECT. But is it really the case that ECT is more severe than complete annihilation? As we will see, there are reasons to think otherwise. And if annihilation is actually a more severe punishment, then we have discovered yet another reason to be skeptical of the traditionalist's claim that infinite human guilt (whether due to infinite human wickedness or divine moral perfection) entails ECT as a just punishment.

Now, it is important to ask, why is it so commonly assumed that ECT is the most severe punishment possible? Probably most people make this assumption because of the *eternality* of the suffering of the damned implied in ECT. What could possibly exceed infinitely long suffering? The first thing to note in response is that the temporal magnitude of ECT is never an *actual* infinity but only a *potential* infinity. Like my baseball-card collection, though the number of moments in the temporal series continues to grow, it is at any given moment finite. So it goes for the suffering of the damned. Stephen Kershnar makes the point as follows: "the amount of suffering a person has undergone is a cumulative property had at a time and there is no time at which a person has had an infinite amount of it."[28] This is because infinity is not reachable through an aggregate of particulars. Therefore, the suffering of the damned, no matter how long they remain in hell, is always finite. So when speaking of ECT, one is always referring to something that is potentially infinite in the sense that it can continue forever—more moments may be added to the series indefinitely. But the series is never actually infinite.[29] This will be important to keep in mind in what follows.

---

28. Kershnar, "Hell and Punishment," 116.

29. This point is generally granted by traditionalists, such as Shawn Bawulski, who says, "while the duration of hell is infinite, it is merely a potential infinity. This is to say that hell's duration is never complete, but rather is one of successive moments, so that time progresses on everlastingly" ("Annihilationism," 76).

Reasons to Think Annihilation is More Severe than ECT

Despite the fact that the suffering experienced by the wicked in ECT is always finite, hell's agonies might be unthinkably painful and horrifying.[30] But it doesn't follow that ECT is the *most* extreme punishment possible nor, importantly, that it constitutes, all things considered, a greater degree of punishment than what is affirmed by conditionalists. On the contrary, there are some considerations that suggest otherwise.[31] Here are three reasons to think that annihilation of the person—even considered independently of psychological torments preceding this—might constitute a more severe punishment than ECT.

First, unlike ECT, *annihilation of the self is complete and final*. The punishment of those who suffer endlessly is neither complete nor final. There is always more suffering to be added to what they have already experienced—more unexecuted divine judgment, more unfulfilled divine wrath. The damnation of the wicked on the conditionalist view is final for all eternity, with personal obliteration providing the most absolute ontological guarantee of its everlasting irreversibility.[32] On the traditional view, although the divine *judgment* may be final and irreversible, the execution of this is not, as cessation of suffering and even potential redemption unto heavenly bliss remain both logical and ontological possibilities. In these respects, the conditionalist conception of damnation appears to be more severe and extreme than that conceived by the traditionalist.[33]

Another reason to regard annihilation of the wicked as a greater degree of punishment than ECT is that it involves *complete removal of goodness in a person*. This can be understood in at least two ways. First, we may

---

30. Some traditionalists are open to the idea that the suffering of the damned is not genuine agony. Thus, they suggest that although the punishment is quantitatively extreme, it need not be qualitatively so. See Crisp, "Divine Retribution," 46 and Bawulski, "Annihilationism," 75–78.

31. Jonathan Kvanvig agrees and calls the belief that annihilation is a mitigation of the traditional view a "delusion." He goes on to offer some historical explanations as to why this misconception is so common. See *Problem of Hell*, 68–69.

32. Conditionalists have sometimes noted that this fact makes better sense—than on the traditional view—of Jesus' statement in Matthew 25:46 that the destruction of the wicked is *aiōnias* (eternal or everlasting). For if the traditionalists are correct, then the wicked are never truly destroyed, since they must be alive and awake in order to experience the torment of hell.

33. For a good biblical exegetical discussion of the finality of the destruction of the wicked, see Bowles, "Revelation 14:11."

consider this in terms of the Augustinian equation of being and goodness. As Augustine says, any existing thing is good so far as it exists. Evil is not a thing or substance in itself but rather a privation of being, a corruption of something that is in itself good.[34] If this is so, then any person suffering in hell, no matter how wicked her conduct on earth or in hell, is good in so far as she is an existing substance. If that is correct, then there is a significant contrast between the traditionalist and conditionalist accounts. According to the former, the state of the person is radically changed in hell, but the goodness of the person as a substance remains. But on the latter view, even the goodness of the person is eliminated. This seems to be a greater degree of punishment. Even some traditionalists have granted this point, as Eleonore Stump does implicitly in claiming that God's keeping the damned in existence is a form of mercy and love.[35]

An alternative theological approach to developing this point about the removal of personal goodness in annihilation would be to explain it in terms of the concept of *imago Dei*. The fact that human beings are made in the image of God, however this is conceived, is something that remains in us so long as we are human. And since (as is agreed by all parties to the debate) the wicked condemned to hell retain their human essence, it follows that they retain at least this significant goodness even as they suffer in agony. But on the conditionalist account, even the *imago Dei* is lost, as the wicked are eventually completely obliterated. For the traditionalist, the image of God in the damned remains forever, but for the conditionalist even this is exterminated. All of their goodness is lost forever. The latter would appear to be a more extreme punishment.

A final reason to think that annihilation is a stronger punishment than ECT is the most basic one of all.[36] Annihilation *eliminates an entire being or substance*, whereas ECT only eliminates: (1) certain *qualities* of that being, viz., positive or pleasant states of consciousness, and (2) some vital *relational* facts and experiences—fellowship with God and any sense of God's (comforting) presence. Even complete and permanent loss of consciousness, while preserving the substance of a human being, would be more severe than ECT, since this would be to eliminate a fundamental goodness

---

34. See *Confessions* 7.12.18. Aquinas makes the same claim in *Summa Theologica*, I.q5.a1 and it is implied in I.q20.a2, where he says, "all existing things, in so far as they exist, are good" (p. 115).

35. See Stump, "Dante's Hell," 181–96.

36. The point I make here is similar in some respects to the first version of the previous point, but it is actually distinct, as I hope my explanation makes clear.

Hell and Divine Goodness

in the person and an essential aspect of her nature. But conditionalism goes farther than this in affirming total annihilation of the being itself, a complete expunging of the person along with all of her qualities and mental states. Otherwise put, the punitive nature of ECT is essentially *qualitative*—pertaining to facts about the person's relational, psychological (and perhaps physical) states, as all or most of her conscious life becomes and remains entirely negative in quality. In contrast, the punitive nature of annihilation is fundamentally *ontological*, pertaining to the condemned person's most basic status as a thing, as she moves from being to absolute nothingness. Again, the latter seems more extreme than the former.

Some Objections

These are significant reasons to think that annihilation of the wicked—whether or not preceded by conscious torment—is a more extreme form of punishment than ECT. This thesis is rarely defended or even discussed in the literature, but some have taken the time to subject it to critique. Thus, Andy Saville appeals to the idea that annihilation itself cannot be infinitely severe because it is not experienced as such. He explains that, "for a punishment to be retributive it must be experienced, but extinction can only be experienced in prospect, and this cannot be a complete apprehension of it in its infinite extent . . . since a finite mind could not fully grasp the prospect of an infinite future, and thus not experience an infinite loss."[37] Shawn Bawulski presents the same objection, as follows: "The only penal aspect related to *annihilation* is the dreadful anticipation of the upcoming annihilation. Yet if the antecedent period of punishment is finite and the anticipatory period of dread is finite, even if the annihilation is permanent and in that sense infinite in consequence, the punishment itself is finite. Thus, I conclude that annihilation should not be considered an infinite punishment."[38] It appears that with this argument Saville and Bawulski beg the question, as they *assume* that the punitive aspect of hell must have entirely to do with the *mental states* of the damned.[39] (Punishment "must be

---

37. Saville, "Arguing with Annihilationism," 73–74. Saville goes on to point out that his reasoning here does not imply that "extinction is not a punishment at all, since the damned may be able to contemplate their coming extinction in a way analogous to that in which a criminal could contemplate their execution in this life" (p. 74).

38. Bawulski, "Annihilationism," 66–67 (emphasis in original).

39. Mark McLeod-Harrison offers the same objection specifically in criticism of my

experienced," insists Saville, and the only thing penal about extinction is "dreadful anticipation," declares Bawulski.) But why assume this? We certainly don't take this view when it comes to earthly punishments. Although a person on death row may experience agonizing dread as she anticipates her execution, such mental anguish is hardly the whole of her punishment. In fact, it doesn't even appear to be a necessary *part* of her punishment. For if a condemned criminal is apathetic or even wants to be executed, so she experiences no dread at all, this doesn't mitigate the fact that her execution is a just punishment for her crime (assuming the moral appropriateness of capital punishment in some cases). The analogy here is admittedly imperfect, but it is enough to show that the justice of a punishment is not entirely contingent upon one's conscious experience of it. It is enough that the person punished loses something valuable (which is the definitive factor on most retributive accounts of punishment). And whether one loses her earthly life or afterlife, these are the most extreme losses a human being can experience in either realm.

Another concern worth addressing here regards a potential implication of the infinitude of annihilation for the conditionalist view. Saville points to what he regards as a redundancy problem that seems to follow for the conditionalist who affirms both that the damned suffer in hell and that this is followed by annihilation. He explains, "if extinction is an infinite punishment, there is a problem of justifying a finite, separate period of torment preceding it. The usual response . . . is that a period of torment allows for different degrees of punishment in hell. However, it remains difficult to see why the difference in finite degrees of torment don't fade

---

view. He writes, "the Spiegelian view of annihilation turns hell into something less than punishment—or less than biblical punishment—for punishment must be conscious" (*Resurrection of Immortality*, 83). This mistaken assumption—that consciousness of the punished person is a necessary condition for genuine punishment—undergirds most of McLeod-Harrison's critique of my arguments (pp. 80-89). Throughout his discussion he questions the legitimacy of any punishment that the person does not experience. Elsewhere, he says, "while the loss of existence, the imago Dei, or substance is a loss, it is not a loss experientially to the one who ceases to be. It remains, however, a loss to the universe, . . . but the annihilated unredeemed . . . has lost nothing because she no longer is a 'she' at all; indeed, she is no longer anything at all." Then, oddly, McLeod-Harrison adds, "so it is with capital punishment. We may call it a punishment, but punishment, if it is to be a punishment of the individual human, seems to require that that *very same individual human* experiences it" (p. 88). Thus, McLeod-Harrison accepts the absurd implication of his view, specifically that capital punishment is not genuine punishment, despite the fact that this contradicts both common sense and Scripture (e.g., Exod 21:12-17; Lev 24:17-22; Num 35:30-31).

into insignificance alongside an *infinite* punishment of extinction."[40] When so cursorily considered, the idea of achieving degrees of punishment by adding varying finite periods of torment to an already infinite punishment certainly seems odd, if not absurd. But Saville too hastily dismisses the idea, which can be salvaged in light of a basic distinction between two kinds of suffering that are involved in any case of punishment. James Cain explains the distinction and applies it to the doctrine of hell:

> The core element of suffering has often been explained in terms of pains of loss and pains of sense. I will distinguish suffering of privation and a positive experiential kind of suffering. One might imagine someone suffering privation without realizing it. If a very young child was injured so that he or she could never develop intellectually beyond a typical four-year-old, that person would suffer a great loss yet might never understand this as a loss, and might be contented and generally cheerful. I take it to be part of the core doctrine of hell that there is a great loss suffered by one in hell, a loss of communion with God and the saints. But I also take it as part of the core doctrine that there is a positive experiential form of suffering. This view is thus incompatible with the view that the loss suffered by the damned merely consists in their being annihilated, and so losing everything that depends on life.[41]

If Cain is correct about the "core doctrine" of hell involving *both* the pains of loss *and* pains of sense, then this suggests a more compelling way for the conditionalist to appeal to degrees of punishment in hell in reply to Saville's redundancy objection, as follows. Although annihilation of the damned is infinite punishment in the ways described above, it is nonetheless limited in the sense that it is but one *form* of punishment, namely the punishment by inflicting loss. Annihilation may be augmented in hell with the punishment of sense, viz. the experience of suffering. And since this is always finite in duration and intensity, this punitive aspect of hell may vary in degrees among the damned. In this way, the conditionalist picture of annihilation preceded by a finite period of torment avoids the redundancy problem. For extinction and the prior torment period serve two distinct retributive functions—the infliction of pain of loss and the infliction of pain of sense, respectively.[42]

---

40. Saville, "Arguing with Annihilationism," 73 (emphasis in original).

41. Cain, "Problem of Hell," 356.

42. To be clear, some conditionalists do not affirm conscious torment of the damned prior to their annihilation in hell, though most do. Such conditionalists might simply

CONDITIONALISM, UNIVERSALISM, AND DIVINE JUSTICE

Above we considered the traditional view of hell as ECT from the standpoint of justice and found that it is deeply problematic, however one attempts to justify it. ECT fails the proportionality criterion whether one assumes 1) that human beings are infinitely wicked, 2) that God is infinitely good, or 3) that human beings continue to sin perpetually in hell. All of these attempts to defend ECT put the traditionalist in the position of having to accept extreme injustices. We have also noted that there are good reasons to be skeptical of the common assumption, shared by traditionalists and non-traditionalists alike, that ECT is a more severe punishment than annihilation. So even if we grant the traditionalist any of the above assumptions such that we must also grant that human beings deserve the most extreme punishment in hell, this still would not entail that ECT is justly proportionate to their guilt. It appears, then, that we have very good reasons to reject traditionalism as a reasonable option when it comes to the justice of hell.

So what about conditionalism and restorationist universalism? Historically, the question of justice has rarely been considered a problem for these views. But it's worth considering some complaints that might be lodged against them. First, regarding conditionalism, some might object that it is unfair for God to destroy human beings. Aquinas, for example, would say that, because of the identification of being and goodness, the eradication of being is always an evil. Regarding this point, Thomist philosopher Eleonore Stump says, "in the absence of . . . an overriding good . . . the annihilation of the damned is not morally justified and thus not an option for a good God."[43] The natural question to pose in response to this argument is, how can avoiding endless suffering and the permanent existence of evil not be an overriding good? Furthermore, since God owns all human beings and brought us into existence, he has the right to destroy some people, particularly those who have persistently rejected and rebelled against him. As the Scriptures say, in comparing God to a potter, he has the right to make some pottery for noble purposes and some for common purposes, including destruction (Rom 9:21–22; Isa 29:16; 45:9).

---

deny that there are degrees of punishment in hell or else account for differences in degree by appealing to some other factor besides suffering, such as a lesser or greater degree of shaming by God at the last judgment.

43. Stump, "Dante's Hell," 196.

Secondly, Wayne Grudem offers this argument from justice against the annihilation of the damned: "Does the short time of punishment envisaged by the annihilationist actually *pay* for all of the unbeliever's sin and satisfy God's justice? If it does not, then God's justice has not been satisfied and the unbeliever should not be annihilated. But if it does, then the unbeliever should be allowed to go to heaven, and he or she should not be annihilated. In either case, annihilation is not necessary or right."[44] Grudem raises an interesting point here about which conditionalists will likely have a variety of responses. Some conditionalists will respond by denying Grudem's assumption that annihilation is actually punitive, in which case the question as to whether the suffering of the damned fully satisfies divine justice is not relevant to the question whether God annihilates the damned. On this view, God punishes the wicked with the suffering they deserve for a determinate period of time and after doing so, he obliterates them. And he may do so because he is under no obligation to sustain them, since they refused the gift of eternal life. Recall the essence of the conditional immortalist thesis, which is that for fallen human beings eternal life is conditional upon our embracing the atoning work of Christ. If the damned never embrace Christ, even after a long period of suffering in hell, then they fail to meet that condition. Therefore, God is not unjust in allowing them to perish. Other conditionalists may take a different approach and insist that annihilation of the wicked is indeed punitive and that the suffering of the damned does not by itself completely satisfy the demands of divine justice. But God imposes the torments of hell on the wicked to varying degrees, depending upon the extent and nature of their earthly rebellion. And the obliteration of their being is the culmination of this punishment.

Another potential non-traditionalist response to Grudem's dilemma would be simply to accept the second option, which is to affirm that after satisfying divine justice by duly suffering in hell for one's sins, the damned are eventually reconciled to God. This is, of course, a version of universalism, and, whatever difficulties might plague this view, biblical or otherwise, it does not appear to be nagged by a justice problem. Indeed, the universalist view seems especially secure from charges of injustice because proponents of this position have at least two conceptual routes to account for the satisfaction of divine justice in the atonement for the sins of the damned. They may take the route just mentioned and say that the damned pay for

---

44. Grudem, *Systematic* Theology, 1151.

their own sins in hell which, to follow Grudem's reasoning, returns them to right standing before God and on this basis they gain eternal life.

The more popular universalist approach, however, would be to say that the atoning work of Christ is what saves all human beings (cf. Rom 5:15–21 and 1 Cor 15:22), and hell serves neither a punitive nor atoning function. Rather, the torments of the damned in hell are God's most extreme chastisement aimed at prompting repentance and the humble surrender of even the most vile rebels. And since the sufferings of Christ are sufficient to atone for an unlimited number and all kinds of sins, there is no injustice in God's applying that atoning work to whomever he wants, however long they have rebelled and regardless of the evils they have done. George MacDonald appears to endorse such a view of the matter when he says, "punishment is for the sake of amendment and atonement. God is bound by His love to punish sin in order to deliver His creature: He is bound by His justice to destroy sin in His creation."[45] And later in the same essay, he writes

> I believe that justice and mercy are simply one and the same thing; without justice to the full there can be no mercy, and without mercy to the full there can be no justice; that such is the mercy of God that He will hold His children in the consuming fire of His distance until they pay the last penny, until they drop the purse of selfishness with all the dross that is in it, and rush home to the Father and the Son, and the many brethren—rush inside the centre of life-giving fire whose outer circles burn. I believe that no hell will be lacking which would help the just mercy of God to redeem His children.[46]

So on MacDonald's view, hell is a divine mercy, the most severe mercy possible, aimed at prompting repentance and ultimately an embrace of the atoning work of Christ, which is the perfect achievement of divine justice.

CONCLUSION

In this chapter, we have considered the doctrine of hell in light of the standard of justice, specifically the proportionality criterion, according to which the severity of a punishment must match the severity of the offense. The discussion focused mainly on the traditional doctrine of hell as eternal

---

45. MacDonald, "Justice," 352.
46. Ibid., 357.

conscious torment, since it is this doctrine which presents the greatest difficulty from the standpoint of justice. We reviewed several options available to traditionalists by which endless suffering might be justified. We found that each of these fails and that extreme injustices are unavoidably entailed by ECT. We also saw that there are good reasons to doubt the common assumption that ECT is a more severe punishment than annihilation, which creates a further problem for traditionalists who affirm ECT because they believe the damned deserve the most extreme sentence possible. Finally, we noted that, in strong contrast to traditionalism, conditionalism and universalism face no significant difficulties when it comes to the matter of justice.

3

Hell and the Problem of Evil

The problem of evil is generally regarded as the most significant philosophical objection to theism and to Christianity in particular. The basic problem is that of reconciling the fact of evil in the world with the omnipotence and goodness of God. If God is all-powerful, then he is *capable* of preventing evil, and if he is perfectly good, then he would *want* to prevent evil. Yet evil is rampant in this world. Many religious skeptics have contended that this is inconsistent with theism, because, as J. L. Mackie argues, "good is opposed to evil, in such a way that a good thing eliminates evil as far as it can, and that there are no limits to what an omnipotent thing can do. From these it follows that a good omnipotent thing eliminates evil completely, and then the propositions that a good omnipotent thing exists, and that evil exists, are incompatible."[1] By "evil," most scholars, including Mackie, would intend what Augustine calls a "privation of good" or any departure from how things ought to be. This includes both *moral* and *natural* evils, as philosophers typically distinguish the two categories. Moral evil refers to any immoral choice or wrongful act performed by a free being, such as lying, stealing, murder, or rape. Natural evil includes suffering that is not the consequence of any intentional action, for example, diseases, birth defects, and bodily injuries, which produce physical pain or psychological trauma to humans or other sentient creatures.

The philosophical problem of evil has been discussed and debated extensively since ancient times, but the doctrine of hell is not typically

---

1. Mackie, "Evil and Omnipotence," 201.

Hell and Divine Goodness

recognized as a part of that problem for Christians. However, increasingly, scholars have begun to identify the problem of hell as a principal aspect of the problem of evil.[2] Any philosophical inquiry into the doctrine of hell, then, should address this problem. In this chapter, we will compare the three major perspectives on hell in terms of their respective capacities for dealing with the problem of evil that the doctrine poses. Since the problem of evil is such a significant philosophical issue, it warrants use as an assessment criterion as we evaluate the three views under discussion.

THE PROBLEM OF EVIL AND THE THREE VIEWS OF HELL

As we consider the three views of hell in light of the problem of evil, for the sake of clarity we will discuss natural and moral evils separately. This will help us to isolate various key issues along the way.

The Problem of Eternal Suffering

It is important to keep in mind that, according to biblical depictions, hell's torments are extremely severe. As we have already noted, in the New Testament hell is described as "a blazing furnace" where there will be "weeping and gnashing of teeth" (Matt 13:42). Other passages similarly liken the experience in hell to being burned alive (Mark 9:43–48; Luke 16:24; Rev 21:8). Whether interpreted literally or figuratively, the torment described would presumably be horribly intense. Other versions of eternal hell are possible, of course, but a properly biblical perspective on the nature of hell is that it involves significant suffering.

Let's assume that for any instance of human suffering allowed or caused by God, there must be some sufficient reason for permitting or causing it. In Scripture we find many grounds for divine allowance of suffering. Such higher ends include the production of joy (1 Pet 4:13); spiritual nourishment (Isa 30:20); maturity and completeness (Jas 1:1–4); purifying

---

2. Some major Christian and atheistic philosophers alike have asserted as much in recent years. Thus, Marilyn McCord Adams has said that "hell poses the principal problem of evil for Christians" ("Problem of Hell," 302). And David Lewis has noted that the problem of hell is the most significant among objections from evil because "the standard versions . . . focus on evil that God fails to prevent," but hell involves "evils that God himself perpetrates" ("Divine Evil," 472).

of faith (1 Pet 1:6–7); perseverance, hope, and character formation (Rom 5:3–4); growth in obedience (Heb 5:8); and sharing Christ's glory (Rom 8:17). In each case there is a higher positive end in view, an ultimate redemptive *point* to the suffering that we experience. In contrast, there can be no redemptive point when it comes to ECT in hell, because for the damned there is nothing *beyond* the suffering.

Here the traditionalist might reply that there *is* a higher end in view when it comes to the eternal suffering of the damned, namely the satisfaction of divine justice. In so far as the wicked receive what they deserve as punishment, that is a positive thing. However, as was made clear in the previous chapter, every version of the doctrine of ECT entails severe injustice. So the route of appeal to justice as a higher end is not available to the traditionalist. Alternatively, then, might there be some other end in view when it comes to ECT that is somehow redemptive? Consider the options available to the traditionalist for making redemptive sense of everlasting suffering. Such ends could be understood in one of three ways, specifically in terms of (a) the damned themselves, (b) non-damned creatures, or (c) God. The problem with the first option, the notion that ECT might be redemptive for the damned, is that, unlike earthly suffering, everlasting torment in hell yields nothing constructive. On the contrary, it is the essence of the concept of ECT that this punishment is utterly non-redemptive for the damned. There is no mercy or escape from the torment on the traditional account.[3] Their suffering never ends, is never diminished, and yields nothing positive for them.

Now consider option (b), which regards the possibility of a redemptive purpose of ECT for *other* creatures (presumably fellow humans, but perhaps also, or instead, angelic beings) who do not go to hell. One might argue that it is redemptive for them to witness the torment of the damned, as this will enable them to better appreciate the power of God as well as their own salvation. As the apostle Paul says, "What if God, choosing to show his wrath and make his power known, bore with great patience the objects of his wrath—prepared for destruction? What if he did this to make the riches of his glory known to the objects of his mercy, whom he prepared

---

3. Even on a modified traditionalist account, which affirms the escapability of hell for some, there would still be people who remain in hell forever and thus for whom there is no redemptive end to their torment. Appeal to escape from hell will only alleviate the problem for the traditionalist if, in the end, all of the damned eventually make their way out of hell. But this is essentially to surrender the doctrine of ECT and embrace universalism.

in advance for glory . . ." (Rom 9:22–23). Granting that the punishment of the wicked can indeed serve to make God's glory known, it is an open question as to what form of punishment this ought to take. Why insist that ECT is necessary for this, as opposed to, say, a finite period of torment followed by annihilation or even ultimate salvation? Why assume that the suffering itself must be everlasting? In fact, as indicated by our discussion in chapter 2, it is not clear that complete annihilation of a human being isn't a *greater* demonstration of the power of God. Accordingly, it might be just as effective in prompting appreciation for one's own salvation. Also, universalists often defend their view in precisely these terms, arguing that final restoration for all is the greatest demonstration of God's power. And in affirming the reality of hell, albeit for limited duration, the universalist may likewise affirm the capacity of hell's torments to effect a greater appreciation for salvation among the redeemed who are graciously spared this experience. Because the traditionalist is the one who affirms everlasting suffering in hell, the burden is on her to show that this is somehow necessary, as opposed to annihilation or restoration of the damned.

Finally, consider option (c), the notion that the redemptive end of ECT has something to do with God. For instance, one might suggest that the redemptive purpose consists in some greater glory to God or deeper satisfaction that God might find in endlessly torturing some of his creatures. As just noted, it is not clear that ECT better contributes to the glory of God than the torment of the wicked followed by either annihilation or restoration. Nor is it clear why this would be more satisfying to God. In fact, given that God is loving and merciful, it seems paradoxical at best to suggest that he would take greater pleasure in sustaining the agony of millions of people for all eternity as opposed to eventually bringing that to a halt. The burden is on the traditionalist to *show* just how this would be more satisfying to God than a period of intense suffering culminating in annihilation or restoration. I am not aware of anyone who has even attempted such an argument, much less plausibly made the case.

Some traditionalists appeal to the venting of the wrath of God as the end served by ECT which satisfies God. Because God is infinitely good, the punishment of the damned must be infinitely great to satisfy the wrath of God. But the satisfaction of divine wrath only makes sense in a context of justice, and this returns us to the justice problem, which vexes traditionalism, as explained in the previous chapter. I will briefly reiterate that argument here as it applies to the context of divine wrath. If the torments of the damned must be infinite in order to achieve ultimate retributive justice and thus satisfy God's wrath, then at no point in the duration of these torments is real justice ever achieved, since never at any point is the penalty fully paid. If retributive justice is never achieved, then God's wrath can never be satisfied. And if God's wrath cannot be satisfied by ECT, then it is difficult to see how God could find the execution of the penalty satisfy*ing*.

It appears, then, that all three of the potential ways that ECT could potentially be redemptive on the traditionalist view are dead ends. There are no compelling reasons to think that ECT could be redemptive either for the damned, for non-damned creatures, or for God in some way that hell followed by annihilation or restoration could not. I conclude that there is *no* sense that ECT could be uniquely redemptive. Clark Pinnock aptly sums up the matter well when he says, "unending torment would be the kind of utterly pointless and wasted suffering which could never lead to anything good beyond it."[4] And gratuitous suffering is entirely out of synch with the portrait of God we find in Scripture.

In sum, then, among the three views of hell, it is the traditional view alone that posits everlasting suffering for the damned. And it is reasonable to suppose that for any instance of human suffering allowed or caused by God, there must be some sufficient reason for permitting or causing it. So the burden is on the traditionalist to provide this sufficient reason, to show how all of this additional post-mortem pain is necessary, as opposed to the limited torment in hell posited by conditionalism and restorationist universalism. Failing this, it would appear that traditionalism affirms the eternal existence of gratuitous suffering. And given that a perfectly good being would never permit this, we have more substantial grounds for thinking traditionalism is false.

The Problem of Eternal Sin

We have noted how ECT creates a problem of unending gratuitous suffering. This is a devastating problem of natural evil for traditionalism. But the traditionalist also faces a problem of unending *moral* evil—sin. In the previous chapter, I explained two aspects of this, depending on the traditionalist's justification for ECT. Given the assumption of the infinite human guilt thesis (IGT)—affirmed either because human characters are infinitely corrupt or because of the status principle (any sin against an infinitely good

---

4. Pinnock, "Destruction," 68.

Hell and Divine Goodness

being creates infinite guilt)—no matter how much the damned suffer in hell, they will forever remain infinitely guilty. Moreover, even if they are incapable of making more sinful choices in this condition, they are nonetheless permanently *sinful*. After all, since they are unredeemed, their natures are just as corrupt as when they lived on earth. Therefore, as long as they exist in hell, sin continues to exist. And, of course, given the traditionalist notion of ECT, this implies that sin exists eternally.

This is a severe problem for the traditionalist who affirms IGT, as the eternality of sin implies that God never gains final victory over sin.[5] Nor does this square with the biblical idea that God will "reconcile all things to himself" (Col 1:20). Yet the problem gets worse. As we noted in the previous chapter, not only does sin exist eternally on their view but *unpunished* sin exists eternally. It is not just that sinners remain in hell forever on the traditional view, but given IGT, there will always be aspects of their sinfulness that remain to be punished. Not only this, but the remaining unpunished sin will always be *infinite*, since no amount of suffering for an infinitely guilty being can reduce the due penalty to a finite point. Note that this will be true of *every* sinner in hell, since each of the damned will be infinitely guilty before God. Therefore, given IGT, *unpunished infinite sin is everlasting*. It is difficult to imagine a scenario where moral evil appears more triumphant than this, where an infinite amount of sin is eternally ineradicable.

As we saw in the previous chapter, many traditionalists appeal to the continuing-sin thesis (CST) to solve the problem. By basing the justification for ECT on the notion that the damned perpetually sin in hell, the traditionalist aims to avoid affirming infinite human sinfulness and the devastating implications for their view this carries with it. Unfortunately for the traditionalist, CST fails to salvage their view. Since the sin of the damned continues forever, and thus always demands more punishment, for all eternity there remains *unpunished* moral evil, specifically the sin currently committed by the damned that next needs to be punished. Presumably, we are to conceive the situation on this model as follows. Suppose

---

5. George MacDonald reflects on this aspect of traditionalism as follows: "Such justice as Dante's keeps wickedness alive in its most terrible forms. The life of God goes forth to inform, or at least give a home to victorious evil. Is He not defeated every time that one of those lost souls defies him? God is triumphantly defeated, I say, throughout the hell of His vengeance. Although against evil, it is but the vain and wasted cruelty of a tyrant. There is no destruction of evil thereby, but an enhancing of its horrible power in the midst of the most agonizing and disgusting tortures a *divine* imagination can invent" ("Justice," 351).

a given person in hell, call her Joy, is suffering for her past sins at time T_1. While Joy is in torment at T_1, she is sinning in some way (such as by not loving God or others with her whole heart and mind), thus requiring more punishment at T_2. While Joy's sins at T_1 are penalized at T_2, she is sinning yet more, thus guaranteeing that she must be further tormented at T_3. And so on, *ad infinitum*. Here we see how there is never a moment in Joy's condemned existence where there is no unpunished sin. While there is no *particular* sin of Joy's for which the punishment remains outstanding throughout eternity, there nonetheless are always some new sins emerging that need to be punished. The sins of the damned are relentlessly fresh and unquenchable. Moral evil, on CST, springs eternal.

So whether the traditionalist opts for IGT or CST, they are saddled with the implication that moral evil remains for all eternity. CST does constitute a mild improvement on IGT, however, for, unlike IGT, CST does not imply that the unpunished human sin that persists eternally is *infinite*. Rather, given CST, there is only finite perpetually unpunished sin for each person in hell. Of course, this is still a devastating problem for the CST-affirming traditionalist, as it still entails eternal moral evil. So either way, the traditionalist is stuck with the implication that unpunished moral evil exists forever. The CST option merely affords the traditionalist the small consolation that this moral evil is not infinite.

Now let's compare this outcome regarding the traditionalist's problem of eternal moral evil to the implications of the non-traditionalist views. Given the conditionalist view, the damned are eventually annihilated. Not only does this put an end to their torment but it also terminates their sinfulness. Since moral evil requires a moral agent, the elimination of the person eradicates the moral evil. Where no moral agent remains, there can be no more guilt, sinfulness, or wrongful choices. So the conditionalist can account for God's final triumph over evil in a way that is consistent with the recurrent biblical theme of the destruction of the wicked and their wickedness. As for God's reconciling all things to himself (Col 1:20), the conditionalist can affirm this in the sense that after the wicked are annihilated, all that remains in existence is fully reconciled to God.

It might appear that the universalist has even less of a problem of moral evil than the conditionalist, since on this view every person in hell eventually repents and Christ's work effectively atones for everyone's sins. In the end, every human being is reconciled to God and no one needs to be perpetually punished or annihilated. But a significant problem remains for the universalist, for there are many fallen angelic beings whose redemption cannot be achieved through Christ's work. What, then, becomes of Satan and his legions of demonic cohorts? If they live forever in torment, then the universalist faces the same unacceptable outcome of eternal moral evil as the traditionalist. But if the universalist grants that all of the fallen angels are annihilated, then this appears to be an unprincipled *ad hoc* escape from the problem. For the universalist has no evidential grounds, biblical or otherwise, by which to justify the claim that only demonic beings are annihilated. This is a serious problem for the universalist.

FREE WILL, SOUL-MAKING, AND THE THREE VIEWS OF HELL

Having established the extent to which each of the three views of hell entails the persistence of natural and moral evil in hell, we are now in a better position to address the problem of evil as it relates to hell, which is this: Why did God make a world in which he knew that many people would go to hell? We will assess each of the three perspectives on hell in terms of how they fare in dealing with this aspect of the problem of evil, which henceforth I will simply refer to as "the problem of hell." To do so, we must consider how some major attempts to justify God's permission of evil are applicable within the context of each view of hell. Among Christian scholars, the two most commonly deployed approaches are the free-will defense and the soul-making theodicy. Others include the punishment theodicy, the aesthetic theodicy, the counterpart theodicy, and the appeal to natural law.[6] In this discussion we will limit our discussion to the free-will and soul-making approaches, and we will do so for two reasons. First, as just mentioned, these are the two most popular responses, and this is likely because they are the two most effective means of dealing with the problem of evil generally. Secondly, the other approaches may be deployed by proponents of each of the three views of hell with equal usefulness. That is, when applying them to the problem of hell, these other theodicies do not reveal significant differences between the three views, unlike the free-will defense and soul-making theodicy, as we will see.

---

6. For defenses of the aesthetic theodicy, see Augustine, *City of God*, XI, 18 and Adams, "Aesthetic Goodness." For a variety of defenses of the natural-laws theodicy, see Swinburne, "Natural Evil," 295–301; Reichenbach, *Evil and a Good God*; 87–120; and DeWeese, "Natural Evil," 53–64.

The Free-Will Defense and the Soul-Making Theodicy

Let's take a closer look at these two major responses to the problem of evil. The free-will defense (FWD)[7] essentially proposes that moral evil is a consequence of human freedom, which God endowed us with for the sake of moral goods and personal relationships. Alvin Plantinga explains the logic of the free-will approach as follows:

> A world containing creatures who are significantly free (and freely perform more good than evil actions) is more valuable, all else being equal, than a world containing no free creatures at all. Now God can create free creatures but He can't *cause* or *determine* them to do only what is right. For if He does so, then they aren't significantly free after all; they do not do what is right *freely*. To create creatures capable of *moral good*, therefore, He must create creatures capable of moral evil; and He can't give these creatures the freedom to perform evil and at the same time prevent them from doing so. As it turned out, sadly enough, some of the free creatures God created went wrong in the exercise of their freedom; this is the source of moral evil.[8]

Some features of this approach are worth highlighting. First, we human beings are entirely to blame for our sin. Though God might have anticipated our rebellion, he did nothing wrong in creating us with the potential for moral evil. It was for our own good that God endowed us with libertarian freedom or what is sometimes called the power of contrary choice. And it is completely our own fault that we have misused this gift. Second, proponents of the FWD place a high premium on self-determination. They regard personal autonomy as so valuable that it justifies the risk of moral evil, though not because of autonomy per se but because it is a crucial

---

7. Since Alvin Plantinga's landmark book *God, Freedom, and Evil*, philosophers of religion have followed his terminological preference in referring to his proposed solution as a "defense" rather than a theodicy. Plantinga explains the distinction as follows: "A theodicist . . . attempts to tell us why God permits evil. Quite distinct from a Free Will Theodicy is what I shall call a Free Will Defense. Here the aim is not to say what God's reason *is*, but at most what God's reason *might possibly be*" (*God, Freedom, and Evil*, 28). A similarly modest approach is possible for those who deploy a soul-making response to the problem of evil, as should become clear in what follows. That is, the soul-making proponent need not insist that she knows what God's reasons for permitting evil *are*. She, too, might prefer to propose what God's reason *might* be.

8. Plantinga, *God, Freedom, and Evil*, 30.

Hell and Divine Goodness

prerequisite for genuinely loving relationships between persons, whether those between human beings or relationships between humans and God.

Like the free-will defense, the soul-making theodicy (SMT) justifies God's permission of evil by appealing to a higher good, and that is character development. While many moral virtues, including kindness, generosity, and love, can be displayed in a world where there is no evil, many other virtues require the existence of sin and/or suffering. These are called "second order" virtues, including such traits as courage, forgiveness, and perseverance. The ancient theologian Irenaeus originated the soul-making theodicy, and John Hick is the most influential contemporary advocate of this approach.[9] As Hick explains it,

> one who has attained to goodness by meeting and eventually mastering temptations, and thus by rightly making responsible choices in concrete situations, is good in a richer and more valuable sense than would be one created *ab initio* in a state either of innocence or of virtue. In the former case, which is that of the actual moral achievements of mankind, the individual's goodness has within it the strength of temptations overcome, a stability based upon an accumulation of right choices, and a positive and responsible character that comes from the investment of costly personal effort.[10]

Proponents of the SMT point out that numerous virtues can only be developed by struggling through difficulties or resisting moral evils. How could one be courageous where there is no danger and nothing to fear? How could sympathy be possible without sorrow or affliction with which to sympathize? How can a person forgive when no one has offended them? Such second-order moral virtues are among the most admirable of all character traits. And, according to Hick and other soul-making proponents, God was morally justified in permitting evil in order to realize these moral goods.

Now it is important to note that although the FWD and SMT are very different in crucial ways, they are also crucially similar insofar as they both propose some good that purportedly makes God's permission of evil worthwhile—genuine relationships and character development.[11] That is,

---

9. See Irenaeus, *Against Heresies*, chapter 38. See also Spiegel, "Irenaean," 80–93.

10. Hick, *Evil and the God of Love*, 255–56.

11. Elsewhere I have argued that the free-will defense and soul-making theodicy are not only complementary approaches to the problem of evil but are actually logically interdependent in the sense that the FWD relies upon some crucial soul-making concepts, while the SMT presupposes a significant notion of human freedom. See Spiegel, "On Free Will," 405–13.

we might say, both justify divine allowance of evil on the basis of a higher good. But the two approaches are also crucially distinct insofar as the FWD assumes a libertarian conception of freedom, while the SMT does not necessarily do so. Those who affirm the libertarian view conceive of freedom as *the power of contrary choice*. This is the idea that a person has acted freely only if given precisely the same circumstances, one could have chosen differently than she actually chose. Thus, libertarians regard free choices nondeterministically. Human freedom and causal determination of choices are incompatible, on their view. In contrast, compatibilists maintain that freedom and determinism are compatible, and they define freedom not in terms of the power of contrary choice but rather as *the power to act according to one's choice*. Thus, for the compatibilist, a person is free if they are able to say or do what they have decided to say or do, even given that their choices and the physical and psychological states that gave rise to them were completely determined by prior causes.

Traditionalism and the Soul-Making Theodicy

Now let's apply the free-will defense and soul-making theodicy to the doctrine of ECT and see if they are of any help in alleviating the traditionalist's problem of hell. First, as to the SMT, we must ask what benefits in terms of character development could arise from everlasting torment of the damned. When it comes to building character through suffering, the only options appear to be that hell could serve a soul-making function for (1) the damned themselves or (2) other human parties, whether people on earth or those who have already arrived in heaven. Obviously, for the eternally damned, no positive character development is possible. Their unending future promises only more pain, misery, and estrangement from God, and no traditionalist would seriously consider the possibility that people in hell become more virtuous through their suffering. On the contrary, most traditionalists would be more inclined to say that life in hell only reinforces such vices as selfishness and hatred toward God.

So what of those still on earth? Might the suffering of the damned somehow serve to build our character here? It is difficult to see how. For one thing, we have too little knowledge of what the damned actually experience, as evidenced by the fact that there is so much debate over the nature of hell. The general understanding that hell is real and that the wicked suffer there might be an effective deterrent from sinful living, but what the traditionalist needs is grounds for thinking that the *eternal* suffering of the damned in particular is useful for such moral goods. Secondly, even if we had specific knowledge both that ECT is true and just what hell's torments involved, this might actually be counter-productive as regards the character development of people on earth. Such knowledge might be as likely to embitter people as to inspire them to virtue, prompting resentment and anger rather than encouraging them to a more godly life.

So, finally, what of those in heaven? Might their character be positively developed somehow through their knowledge of ECT? Again, this is highly doubtful, firstly, because the redeemed in heaven are already morally perfected through what theologians call the process of glorification. Whether this happens instantaneously, in the "twinkling of an eye," as Paul says in 1 Corinthians 15:52, or through a gradual process, such as through purgatorial purification,[12] Christians are perfected in their humanity so no moral growth is needed. In response, a traditionalist might propose that it is partly through knowledge of the suffering of the damned that this final purification in heaven is achieved. However, this is counter-intuitive since a much-debated problem related to ECT concerns how knowledge of the torments of loved ones in hell would seem to undermine the joy of the blessed in heaven. As we will see in chapter 5, a popular way of dealing with that problem is to propose that the memories of the damned will be expunged from the minds of the redeemed, the tacit assumption of this theory being that awareness of the suffering of those in hell is not helpful but harmful. Anyway, it is difficult to see how knowledge of the ECT of the damned would be a greater moral benefit to the redeemed than knowledge that those in hell suffer severely but temporarily.

Traditionalism and the Free-Will Defense

So it appears that the SMT is useless for the traditionalist as a way of dealing with the problem of hell. Next, let's consider the free-will defense. Perhaps the most well-known appeal to human free will in this context is that of C. S. Lewis, who says, "in creating beings with free will, omnipotence from the outset submits to the possibility of . . . defeat. . . . I willingly believe that the damned are, in one sense, successful, rebels to the end; that the doors

---

12. I have in mind the view affirmed by Roman Catholics and perhaps supported by such passages as 1 Corinthians 3:11–15.

of hell are locked on the inside."[13] Thus, on this view, the miseries of hell are self-imposed rather than forced upon the wicked. But does this get God off the moral hook, considering that hell's torments are everlasting and God presumably knew in advance that this would be the consequence of his creating human beings with libertarian freedom? Those who affirm the simple foreknowledge view of divine providence (SF) would certainly say so. Jacob Arminius, for example, asserts that "the understanding of God is certain and infallible; so that he sees certainly and infallibly, even things future and contingent, whether he sees them in their causes or in themselves."[14] John Wesley likewise affirmed SF, even in the context of free human choices: "God *foreknew* those in every nation who would believe, from the beginning of the world to the consummation of all things."[15]

Proponents of SF maintain that God exhaustively foreknows all events of history, including the free choices of human beings, and that God sovereignly governs the world based on this foreknowledge. By recognizing that God's foreknowledge is logically prior to his decrees for history, SF aims to preserve human libertarian freedom.[16] Thus, the traditionalist who affirms SF might say that although God foreknew that many people would ultimately go to hell and suffer ECT, God did not predetermine this. Moreover, she might insist that God was willing to create a world in which this would happen only because he knew that, on the whole, it would be the best world overall.

Setting aside the "best world" hypothesis for now (we will revisit this below), the SF view has serious problems even independently of its application to the problem of hell. First, as has often been noted, SF reduces to a deterministic view, since God's knowledge of the future is complete and incorrigible from the moment he creates the world. Therefore, from the standpoint of divine providence, given SF, God's initial creation of the world is tantamount to his predetermination of the *entirety* of human history. So how could the SF view even be consistent with libertarian human freedom? Secondly, in attempting to shield human freedom, the SF view actually inhibits divine freedom, making God's providential control redundant or vacuous. As William Hasker has pointed out, given SF, "it is clear that God's foreknowledge cannot be used either to *bring about* the

---

13. Lewis, *Problem of Pain*, 127.
14. Arminius, "Disputation 17," 37.
15. Wesley, "On Predestination," 417 (emphasis in original).
16. For a recent exposition of this view, see Hunt, "Divine Providence," 394–414.

occurrence of a foreknown event or to *prevent* such an event from occurring.... In the logical order of dependence of events, one might say, by the 'time' God knows something will happen, it is 'too late' either to *bring about* its happening or to *prevent* it from happening."[17]

Perhaps an open theist perspective might provide help for the traditionalist here. Open theists are motivated by a general concern to shield God from responsibility for human evil, and they do so by *denying* exhaustive divine foreknowledge. Richard Creel writes, "God always knows exhaustively what the future can be, and he always knows what it will be insofar as it is completely determined by his will.... However, insofar as what he wills is alternatives for free creatures to choose between or among, God does not know which of the alternatives will come to pass."[18] This amounts to what John Sanders and others dub a "risk" model of providence. God controls and determines much of creation, but out of respect for human freedom, he leaves our choices up to us so that human history could go any of an infinite number of directions, and this includes how many people will be redeemed and how many will ultimately end up in hell. Open theists generally recognize that their view entails the possibility that God's risks in creation might turn out to have been less than wise. Thus, Sanders can seriously ask, "Is God a fool? Will his attempts at restoration succeed? Sanders' answer: "Only the history of God's activity and the human response to it will tell."[19] And elsewhere he admits, "sometimes God's plans do not bring about the desired result and must be judged a failure."[20] These are remarkable and, in one sense, admirably forthright concessions. But they are also deeply problematic. Biblically speaking, the view is untenable since Scripture repeatedly and emphatically affirms exhaustive divine foreknowledge (e.g., Ps 139:4; Isa 42:9; 46:10; Jer 1:5; Acts 2:23; 3:18; Rom 8:29).[21]

But there are also philosophical problems with the open theists' risk model of providence, especially as this applies to the problem of hell. According to open theists, the miseries of ECT are not known by God in advance, so this exonerates God in his permitting impenitent humans to go to hell. But does it really? Given libertarian free will, it would have been

---

17. Hasker, *God, Time, and Knowledge*, 57–58.
18. Creel, *Divine Impassibility*, 98–99.
19. Sanders, *God Who Risks*, 49.
20. Ibid., 88.
21. For extensive theological critiques of open theism, see Frame, *No Other God*; Spiegel, *Benefits of Providence*, 19–78; Ware, *God's Lesser Glory*.

possible that the overwhelming majority of—or even *all*—human beings would be damned to ECT. This seems far too risky a venture for a perfectly good God to accept. Even if God were justified in initially risking hell for human beings, such that he might reasonably allow the first few impenitent people to be eternally damned, why think that this justifies God in continuing to allow *millions* of others to follow the same fate over thousands of years of human history? And why not do more to intervene and make their choices better informed? Thus, after the pattern of damnation went into full swing in early human history, presumably God would have anticipated that this pattern would continue, even if he lacks exhaustive foreknowledge, as open theists maintain. Thus, open theism seems to be no better than the simple divine foreknowledge approach when it comes to deploying the FWD in dealing with the problem of hell.

A far more promising option for the traditionalist is the Molinist version of the FWD, and the most well-known recent application of this to the problem of hell is that of William Lane Craig. First devised by the sixteenth-century theologian Luis de Molina (hence "Molinism"),[22] this approach proposes that God's knowledge of human history is not simple divine foreknowledge but what Molina calls "divine middle knowledge"— God's counterfactual knowledge of what free creatures *would* do in all possible worlds. In planning his creation of the world, God consulted his middle knowledge and chose to instantiate that world that was best overall. Thus, our world, despite all of its suffering and sin, is actually the best of all possible worlds containing libertarian free creatures.

Craig applies this Molinist perspective to the doctrine of hell in order to defend the traditional doctrine of ECT. Other things being equal, God would prefer a world in which all people are saved to a world in which some are condemned to hell. But given the libertarian freedom of human beings, it was impossible to make such a world. At best, many would be saved but not all. Thus, as Craig puts it, "an omnibenevolent God might want as many creatures as possible to share salvation; but given certain true counterfactuals of creaturely freedom, God, in order to have a multitude in heaven, might have to accept a number in hell."[23] But why would God have to accept that? Surely an omnipotent being could avoid such a concession to eternal misery. Craig's response is that it might be the case that for some people there are no possible worlds in which they *freely* submit to

22. See Molina, *Divine Foreknowledge*.
23. Craig, "No Other Name," 182.

God. Thus, Craig's suggestion is that some persons would freely reject God regardless of the circumstances in which they were placed. Such people suffer from what Craig calls "transworld damnation."[24] Consequently, according to Craig, it might be the case that in order to have a world where a significant number of people find salvation there would necessarily also be many people who are lost. Thus, he says, for all we know, "the balance between the saved and lost in the actual world is . . . an optimal balance."[25]

Craig's Molinist version of the FWD regarding hell is innovative, but does it ultimately succeed? First, we may ask, is the good of having a large number of people in heaven really worth the cost of a large number of people suffering eternally in hell? Craig assumes without argument that it is, but there are good reasons to be doubtful. In ordinary human experience, we would not allow for the perpetual suffering of even one child for the sake of the happiness of a large community.[26] We would consider this to be heartless utilitarian reasoning. So why suppose that a morally perfect God would deign to such crude cost-benefit analysis? If it would be immoral to permit even one person to suffer severely for the happiness of a large community, then how much more absurd is the idea that God would allow *millions* of people to suffer eternally in order to have an equally large number of people experience eternal happiness?[27]

Next, consider Craig's concept of transworld damnation—the notion that some people would freely reject God regardless of their life circumstances. If we assume libertarian free will, then on what grounds should we have any confidence in this? Indeed, the very notion of libertarian freedom—where to be free is to enjoy the power of contrary choice—seems to entail that there is no way to know in advance of a person's choosing

---

24. Craig's notion of "transworld damnation" is indebted to Alvin Plantinga's concept of "transworld depravity." See Plantinga, *Nature of Necessity*, 184–89.

25. Craig, "'No Other Name,'" 183.

26. In her award-winning short story "The Ones Who Walk Away from Omelas" Ursula K. Le Guin powerfully illustrates such a situation with the aim of demonstrating how morally ludicrous is the utilitarian justification of human suffering as a means of achieving immense pleasures for others—precisely the sort of reasoning that Craig employs with his Molinist free-will defense.

27. Even if we accept the utilitarian calculus implicit in Craig's reasoning, why should we suppose that God would *want* to make this choice given the sorrow it would cause God, assuming he loves those he damns? Thus, Thomas Talbott asks, "one wonders why Craig thinks it even possible that God would willingly make himself *eternally* miserable? Does God really have so little regard for *himself* as that?" ("Craig on the Possibility," 498).

exactly what they will choose.²⁸ As Stephen Kershnar has pointed out, the concept appears to undermine the notion that the transworld damned are truly free and responsible in every world. Such people, Kershnar observes, "cannot be damned in every world in which they exist, since this would be true only if their rejection of God's grace followed from their essential nature and this would so greatly restrict their act-options as to undermine their responsibility for rejecting God's grace."²⁹ That is to say, in order to be certain that a particular person would always reject God, there would need to be determining factors within the person guaranteeing this. Thus, Craig's reasoning is implicitly reliant on determinism, which contradicts the very free-will defense he is using.

Kershnar makes another critical observation about Craig's argument which pertains to a problematic dilemma it raises. Either Craig must assume that individual decisions to submit to God are causally linked to one another or they are not. If they are linked, "then the linkage would undermine responsibility and hence the basis for sending or allowing someone to go to hell."³⁰ But if they are not linked, then there is a possible world in which there are no transworld damned, since God would then be able to simply subtract those potential human beings from the world he makes. And this means that God *can* make a world in which every inhabitant is saved. So Craig must either surrender the libertarian conception of human freedom or give up the notion that human freedom is incompatible with universal salvation.

Thus far in our critical assessment of Craig's free-will defense, we have been considering its usefulness for traditionalism generally. But it will be helpful to consider a particular problem related to its application to the CST version of traditionalism. One of the debates in the hell literature concerns the very possibility of someone rejecting God forever. Thomas Talbott has argued that it is not even possibly true that some people could freely and irrevocably reject God despite his best efforts to save them.³¹ After all, there is no reasonable motive that a person could have to consistently resist recon-

---

28. This objection actually targets the root of Craig's argument, which is his assumption that God could have counter-factual knowledge of libertarian free choices. The key problem is that, being counter-factual, such knowledge cannot possibly be grounded in anything. Hence, this is called the "grounding problem" of Molinism. See Adams, "Middle Knowledge," 109–17 and Cowan, "Grounding Objection," 93–102.

29. Kershnar, "Injustice of Hell," 118.

30. Kershnar, "Hell and Punishment," 123.

31. Talbott, "Providence, Freedom, and Human Destiny," 227–45.

ciling to God, and if their resistance was based in ignorance or deception, then God, being almighty, would easily be able to remove that ignorance or shatter the illusions that are hindering their submitting to God. And being perfectly good, God would want to remove all such obstacles to redemption. Raymond VanArragon has challenged Talbott's reasoning by suggesting that at least in some cases God's taking the necessary steps to ensure a person's salvation, such as through the removal of a recalcitrant sinner's desire to sin, would constitute an imposition on their freedom, so in such cases even God could not guarantee that a person would freely choose redemption.[32] Whatever the truth might be regarding this debate and the possibility of a person rejecting hell forever, given CST, it actually misses the point when it comes to the free-will defense of traditionalism. For the crucial question is not whether some person or other might possibly reject God forever but rather whether it is possible that *all* of the (presumably millions of) people in hell could freely reject God forever. That is a far different claim and, it seems to me, an indefensible one. For if God can successfully draw so many millions of sinners to himself for reconciliation during their earthly lives, then couldn't he succeed in doing so at least occasionally with those in hell? A way out for the traditionalist here, of course, would be to concede that escape from hell is possible, though that would be a departure from the standard traditionalist position.

So the Molinist free-will defense of traditionalism appears to be no more helpful to the traditionalist than the open theist and simple divine foreknowledge versions of the FWD. When it comes to doctrines of providence and divine foreknowledge, the remaining option is the Augustinian-Calvinist view, which affirms an alternative view of freedom, namely compatibilism. As noted earlier, on this view freedom is not the power of contrary choice but the ability to act according to one's choices, which are themselves determined by prior factors, such as a person's character and psychological states, which in turn are determined by other contingencies and, ultimately, God's sovereign decrees. On this view, there really is no FWD available, since God predetermines human fates from all eternity. In fact, the Augustinian-Calvinist view of providence only seems to make matters worse for traditionalism, since it implies a doctrine of double predestination: God foreordains the elect to heaven and everyone else to hell to suffer ECT.[33] The damned, as it were, never really had a chance to

32. VanArragon, "Is It Possible to Freely Reject God Forever?"
33. As the *Westminster Confession of Faith* plainly asserts, "some men and angels are

be redeemed. They were created by God, on this view, for the purpose of ultimate damnation in the form of everlasting suffering and, depending on whether one accepts CST, perhaps also for everlasting rebellion. Augustinian-Calvinism, therefore, offers no solution to the problem of eternal evil plaguing the traditionalist.

Conditionalism, the Free-Will Defense, and the Soul-Making Theodicy

I conclude, then, that neither the FWD nor SMT are of any help in salvaging the traditional view of hell as eternal conscious torment. Now let us consider whether or to what extent these approaches may be useful for the conditionalist account of hell. First, it is important to clarify that because on this view the damned are annihilated after a fixed period of suffering, the problem of hell facing the conditionalist is infinitely less severe than that facing the traditionalist (because eternity is infinitely longer than any finite period of time). Still, the torments of hell and the obliteration of human beings are significant evils that demand moral justification.

The FWD might be of some use for the conditionalist. As noted, the natural and moral evils accruing for the damned are infinitely less than those on the traditional view, and this dramatically changes the cost-benefit calculus. On the traditional view, the eternal misery of the damned is supposed to be offset and even overcome by the eternal joy of the redeemed in heaven. For some, such as William Lane Craig, this makes intuitive sense, but for many others, including myself, it is counter-intuitive, even morally abhorrent. But if conditionalism is true, it is only *finite* misery of the damned—which always approximates the severity of their sins, thus satisfying the proportionality criterion of justice—that must be offset by the everlasting joy of the redeemed in heaven. This is a far more plausible prospect which could save the FWD for the conditionalist. This fact, in turn, greatly reduces the problems attending the concept of transworld damnation discussed above, since that damnation is constituted by a just finite period of suffering followed by annihilation. And this annihilation of the damned is properly understood as simply a return of the wicked to the nothingness from which they came, a natural consequence of their

---

predestined unto everlasting life, and others foreordained to everlasting death" (section 3.3).

libertarian free choice to reject God or the fact that it never was God's will for them to live forever (depending on one's view of divine providence).

So the FWD holds some promise for the conditionalist in dealing with the problem of hell. Nevertheless, it seems to me that the FWD remains problematic in its own right and is not an ultimate solution to the problem of hell facing the conditionalist. As for the SMT, the character-building benefits of hell seem no more promising on the conditionalist view than on the traditional view, whether for the damned themselves or those still on earth. As for the redeemed in heaven, the final termination of the damned might at least relieve some of the difficulty of the problem of depleting the joy of those in heaven because of the misery of lost loved ones. This will be addressed in detail in chapter 5.

However, we need not conclude from the fact that the FWD and SMT are not very helpful for conditionalists that they are necessarily saddled with a severe problem of evil related to their view of hell. The conditionalist can appeal to the *justice* of the punishment of hell, as the damned suffer just as much as they deserve and then are annihilated. (Such final justice is impossible on the traditional view, as we have seen.) For the conditionalist, then, consummate eschatological justice could conceivably alleviate the problem of evil to the extent that appeals to the FWD and SMT or any other theodicy are unnecessary.

Universalism, the Free-Will Defense, and the Soul-Making Theodicy

How useful are the FWD and SMT for universalism? In addressing this question, it is of course crucial to keep in mind that on the universalist view all are redeemed in the end. So all suffering and sin are temporary, but all joy is eternal. The eternality of joy is true as a *general* fact for conditionalism, too, but for universalism it is true for *every individual* human being.

First, consider the FWD for universalism. On this view, the cost-benefit calculus in favor of God's including hell in his plans for the world becomes far more compelling. Given universalism, hell is neither a perpetual torture chamber nor a painful preface to obliteration but is rather comparable to a painful surgical procedure, where the temporary suffering, however severe and even if long in duration, is more than compensated for by the eternal benefits for the redeemed. Also, for the universalist the FWD alleviates the problem of transworld damnation for the Molinist, because no one's condemnation lasts forever. Other problems inherent to the FWD remain, of course, but to the extent that it is useful at all in dealing with the problem of hell, it will be of the most help to the universalist.

As for the SMT, there are potentially significant benefits of hell on the universalist view. For the damned, hell may serve a *soteriological* function, prompting repentance and final surrender to and reconciliation with God. Hell may also serve a *sanctifying* function on the universalist view, as hell effectively purges sin and rebellion from the wicked, perhaps even enabling them to personally experience the psychological effects of their sin on other people. Thus the damned may grow in terms of sorrow and hatred for sin, empathy for others, and especially humility and a sense of justice and the interconnectedness of humanity. These are all moral traits that, upon their restoration to God and fellow human beings, would result in a more mature and virtuous moral character which can positively contribute to the fellowship of the redeemed.[34]

For those on earth, again, the lack of knowledge regarding the nature of hell limits the soul-making benefits of universalism. But to the extent that one could be confident that universalism was true, this would no doubt be encouraging to friends and family members of the damned, knowing that their rebellious loved ones would not be lost forever. On the other hand, such knowledge might also ultimately undermine moral seriousness on earth. The power of the doctrine of hell to deter wickedness on earth should not be underestimated, despite the fact that this aspect of the doctrine is often critiqued and even parodied. Human beings are naturally deterred by the prospect of potential negative, painful consequences of their actions. And it would seem this applies at the eschatological level as well as in our daily lives.

If universalism is true and all people are ultimately saved, might this explain the ambiguity of the biblical record regarding the nature and extent of hell, as we saw in the first chapter? After all, if permanent damnation— whether in the form of ECT or annihilation—creates a stronger deterrent to sin and motivation to live rightly, then there would be some utilitarian value in people thinking that such a fate was at least possible, if not likely, for the wicked. Some are sure to object here, however, that this would amount to a form of divine deception and God would never mislead us in Scripture.

---

34. For some helpful discussions of the problem of evil from a universalist perspective, see MacDonald (Parry), *Evangelical Universalist*, 157–62 and Kronen and Reitan, *God's Final Victory*, 187–91.

In response, first, I would not characterize Scripture's ambiguity regarding the nature of hell as divine deception but, at most, a form of concealment.[35] And there are plenty of instances of divine concealment in Scripture, relating to everything from such critical doctrines as the divine Trinity (which is not unveiled until the New Testament and even here must be arrived at through careful systematic theology) and the divinity of Christ (which Jesus himself concealed during his time on earth) to significant truths related to church-state relations, charismatic gifts, the role of women in the church, and diverse other issues that have been debated for the entire history of Christianity. Presumably, such biblical ambiguities or concealments were intended by God for our good. So in the case of Scripture's teaching on hell, it seems reasonable to suppose that God had good reasons to conceal the full truth of the issue, one of which could regard maximizing human motivation to live rightly. So the idea that God would conceal the truth of universal salvation (if such were true) in Scripture to prevent apathy regarding the moral life is not far-fetched but has some precedent in biblical revelation.[36]

CONCLUSION

In this chapter, we have addressed a variety of issues related to the problem of evil posed by the doctrine of hell. Recall that our primary purpose in this discussion was to compare the three major perspectives on hell in terms of their respective capacities for dealing with the problem. We found that on the traditional view of hell there is a two-fold problem of eternal evil. There is eternal natural evil in the form of suffering experienced by the damned who are subject to ECT, and there is also eternal moral evil, as the damned either are infinitely guilty (IGT) or sin perpetually in hell (CST). In

---

35. Even if one were to grant that this does imply a sort of divine deception, it can be pointed out that biblical revelation presents us with other cases of divine deceptions, including God's commanding Abraham to sacrifice Isaac (Gen 22:1–14), God's commanding the Hebrew mid-wives' deception in Exodus 1:15–21, God's use of a deceiving spirit to deceive Ahab (1 Kgs 22:19–23), and instances where God uses deception to ensnare Israel's enemies in battle (e.g., Josh 8:1–9).

36. Of course, some will insist that the biblical record is far from ambiguous when it comes to the doctrine of universalism but rather rules it out conclusively. However, the fact that throughout church history major biblical scholars and theologians have thought otherwise, and in many cases even thought that the Bible conclusively favors universalism, ought to give one pause regarding such confidence.

both cases, moral evil is everlasting, but on IGT, that moral evil is infinite. Next we considered whether and to what degree the two major approaches to the problem of evil—the free-will defense and the soul-making theodicy—might be helpful for each of the three views on hell. We saw that for the traditionalist, the SMT provides no help, as neither the damned themselves nor other human parties, whether those earth or those in heaven, stand to benefit morally from the eternal torment of the damned. As for the FWD, we found that no version of this approach, whether cast in the context of simple divine foreknowledge, open theism, or Molinism, provides significant help to alleviate the traditionalist's problem of hell. As regards conditionalism, we found that the SMT is of no more help than it is for traditionalism, but the FWD is a somewhat more promising approach for conditionalism if only because the problem of hell is infinitely less severe for conditionalism than for the traditional view. And given the finitude of human suffering in hell, this makes the free-will defender's utilitarian justification for hell more plausible on the conditionalist view. Finally, in the context of universalism, we saw that both the FWD and the SMT are highly useful for dealing with the problem of hell. The temporary nature of human suffering along with the promise of universal salvation justify God's risking damnation by giving humans libertarian freedom. And there is significant character development justification of hell in the soteriological and sanctifying functions it may serve for the damned.

The upshot of this part of our study, then, is that the traditional view of hell suffers from an especially severe problem of evil related to hell, as compared to the non-traditional views. And although the FWD and SMT are more helpful to the universalist than the conditionalist, it doesn't follow that conditionalism suffers from a worse problem of evil than universalism *overall*, since the *justice* of the limited suffering and annihilation of the damned can potentially alleviate the problem of hell for the conditionalist, perhaps to the same extent that the ultimate redemption of the damned can do so for the universalist.

4

Hell, Immortality, and Salvation

To this point in our inquiry into the comparative philosophical merits of the three views of hell, we have focused on issues related to justice and the problem of evil. We have found that the traditional doctrine of hell as eternal conscious torment fares very poorly when it comes to these issues. In this chapter we will explore some issues related to human immortality and salvation which reveal significant problems with the universalist perspective.

ON IMMORTALITY

A point of agreement between traditionalists and universalists is their belief that all human beings are immortal. Thus, generally speaking, proponents of both views reject the view that immortality is conditional upon a person's salvation. The disagreement between them concerns not whether human beings live forever but rather what *condition*—torment or blessedness—characterizes their everlasting life. But what philosophical grounds are there for believing that human beings are naturally immortal? Let us consider some important philosophical arguments that have been deployed in defense of this claim.[1]

An early defense of the natural immortality of the soul appears in Plato's *Phaedo*. In the dialogue, Socrates presents no fewer than four arguments

---

1. For a good theological critique of the doctrine of the natural immortality of the soul, see Hughes, "Is the Soul Immortal?"

Hell, Immortality, and Salvation

in defense of the claim that he will survive his impending death. In doing so, he appeals to natural cycles, a doctrine of knowledge as recollection (thus supposedly proving soul transmigration), and a quirky argument from the doctrine of forms. None of these arguments reasons on the basis of the nature of the soul itself, but a fourth argument he gives apparently does so, which might explain why it has been historically more influential than the other three arguments. This argument appeals to the idea that the soul is a simple substance. First, Socrates observes that the soul is opposite the body in many respects. The body is visible, variable, tangible, etc., while the soul is invisible, invariable, intangible, etc. And since the body is also divisible, subject to being broken into parts, it stands to reason that the soul is *indivisible*—being a simple substance that has no parts. Given these opposite qualities, Socrates suggests that it is "natural for body to disintegrate rapidly, but for soul to be quite or very nearly indissoluble."[2] And since the soul is indissoluble, it is naturally resistant to destruction, which is to say, the soul naturally survives death. This has become known as the argument from simplicity, and versions of the argument were later defended by Plotinus and Leibniz.

While intriguing, the argument from simplicity fails to prove that all human souls live forever. For one thing, even if the soul is naturally immortal, in the sense that, other things being equal, a given person will live forever, this does not rule out the possibility that God might overcome the soul's natural tendency toward persistence. Just because a soul is a simple substance and thus insusceptible to being broken down into component parts, it doesn't follow from this that it is utterly indestructible. For presumably God can destroy a soul (as Jesus notes in Matthew 10:28) by annihilating it altogether.[3] Natural immortality, then, does not imply absolute indestructibility.[4]

---

2. Plato, *Phaedo*, 63.

3. Though himself a proponent of the simplicity argument for the soul's immortality, Leibniz granted this much about the soul's susceptibility to destruction by God. Regarding the duration of souls, he writes, "since every *simple substance* which possesses a true unity can have its beginning and end by miracle alone, it follows that they could not begin except by creation, nor come to an end except by annihilation" (*Philosophical Writings*, 117).

4. Despite Socrates' and Plato's failure to demonstrate that human souls are naturally immortal, this doctrine has nonetheless profoundly influenced Western thinking on the subject for millennia. As Clark Pinnock has said, "belief in the natural immortality of the soul which is so widely held by Christians, although stemming more from Plato than the Bible, really drives the traditional doctrine of hell more than exegesis does"

Thomas Aquinas developed a distinct but related argument for the immortality of the soul, reasoning from the metaphysical nature of the soul to the conclusion that it is indestructible. Beginning with the notion that the soul is a subsistent form, not dependent on the body for any of its activities, Aquinas reasons that "the human soul could not be corrupted unless it were corrupted *per se*," but "it is impossible for a form to be separated from itself; and therefore it is impossible for a subsistent form to cease to exist."[5] It follows that a human soul cannot cease to exist. Aquinas' argument appears to be formally valid. The problem, however, is that by assuming that the soul is a subsistent form he packs into his major premise the notion of immortality. So the argument actually begs the question. In any case, even if Aquinas' argument succeeded in showing the human soul to be *naturally* immortal it remains possible that God could destroy the soul *supernaturally*.[6] Thus, Aquinas' argument is really of no more use in demonstrating the necessary immortality of the soul than is Socrates' simplicity argument.

So a major problem plaguing the arguments from Plato and Aquinas pertains to their failure to address the matter of the divine will to preserve or ultimately destroy human souls. Mark McLeod-Harrison has recently developed an innovative philosophical defense of natural immortality that avoids this pitfall, so it is worth considering in some depth. His argument fundamentally features a challenge to the common assumption that God owns human beings. McLeod-Harrison appeals to what he calls "structural value"—those values, such as beauty and justice, which are imbedded in the "normative world." Like the values of justice and beauty, the structural value of human beings is communal in the sense that it is owned by no one in particular, not even God. McLeod-Harrison proceeds to argue that "causing something with structural value to cease to exist is bad." And since humans are structurally valuable, "God's causing the soul-cessation of humans, even though God created them, is a bad thing."[7]

What constitutes the structural value of human beings, McLeod-Harrison says, is our "robust free will," the fact that we are "self-determining

---

("Destruction," 66).

5. Aquinas, *Summa Theologica*, 368.

6. As Frederick Copleston notes, Aquinas seems only to show that the soul's "immortality follows from its nature and is not simply gratuitous." Still, "it could, of course, be annihilated by the God who created it" (*History of Philosophy*, 384).

7. McLeod-Harrison, *Resurrection of Immortality*, 37.

things."[8] Here McLeod-Harrison intends not only libertarian free will, but the sort of freedom that also implies divine risk in creating us, since it entails the possibility of evil. McLeod-Harrison concludes that God would never destroy a human soul since this would be "to challenge the structural nature of love that God built into the universe. God doesn't destroy human souls because God can't metaphysically do so. The metaphysics of the world is good, structured by love. To remove the thing that allows for love in a human is to disvalue the very structure of the world."[9] McLeod-Harrison describes human immortality as a "strongly enduring property," that is, the sort of property "such that once one has them, there is no time one doesn't have them."[10] Because it is irrevocable, humans may be said to possess "immutable immortality." Consistent with his view of providence, he insists that God takes a "hands-off policy" when it comes to human choices.

The premise that human beings are self-determining is the key guiding assumption in McLeod's central argument for immutable human immortality. Here is his "Master Argument" in full:

1. All other things being equal, if an event interferes with a human h's freedom, the event is metaphysically bad. (Premise)
2. An event leading to the permanent cessation of human h is an event that interferes with h's freedom. (Premise)
3. Therefore, an event leading to the permanent cessation of a human h is metaphysically bad. (1, 2)
4. Some metaphysically bad events would undermine the divine nature were they to occur. (Premise)
5. It is impossible for events to occur that would undermine the divine nature. (Premise)
6. The permanent cessation of a human is a metaphysically bad event that undermines the divine nature. (Premise)
7. Therefore, the permanent cessation of a human is impossible. (3, 4, 5, 6)

If successful, McLeod-Harrison's argument demonstrates that all human beings must live forever—in some condition or other. As for whether any

8. Ibid., 39.
9. Ibid., 42.
10. Ibid., 52.

humans suffer everlasting torment in hell or universalism is true, he observes that "natural immortality is neutral in that regard,"[11] though judging by some favorable remarks he makes about the ideas of (universalist) Thomas Talbott, it appears that McLeod-Harrison at least leans in a universalist direction.

What are we to make of this argument? First, McLeod-Harrison's methodology is thoroughly philosophical and does not incorporate scriptural exegesis. Generally speaking, this is all well and good, but there are some critical junctures in his argument where the discussion really begs for some exegetical input. For example, such passages as Acts 17:28 ("in him we live and move and have our being"), Romans 9:20–21 (which compares humans to clay used by a potter), and 1 Corinthians 6:19–20 ("you are not your own; you were bought at a price"), not to mention the entire Genesis creation account, are directly relevant to the whole matter of divine ownership of human beings. These passages, as well as numerous other biblical texts, suggest a strong sense of divine ownership of human beings, which undermines McLeod-Harrison's argument. Specifically, divine ownership of humans seems to show that, with regard to the *ceteris paribus* clause of premise 1, other things are *not* equal when it comes to God's interference with human freedom, so such divine interference in the form of destroying a human soul is not necessarily metaphysically bad. This would furthermore seem to show that, vis-à-vis premise 6, such destructive divine interference would not necessarily undermine the divine nature.

Secondly, in assuming that human beings are entirely self-determining, McLeod-Harrison forecloses in favor of a particular libertarian view of human freedom. For all we know, libertarianism is false and a compatibilist view of human freedom is the correct view. Now this libertarian assumption, along with the presumption of an open theist view of providence, are critical to his argument. So the argument will only be useful for readers who share these views. But, as we will see below, these very assumptions further restrict McLeod-Harrison's sympathetic audience, since they arguably rule out universalism. If human beings are entirely self-determining, then there is no way for God to *guarantee* (that is, determine) that all people will ultimately submit to him for redemption. McLeod-Harrison suggests that God may "remove all limitations" so that the "only rational choice is to move toward God."[12] However, if people are truly self-determining and

---

11. Ibid., 26.

12. McLeod-Harrison, *Resurrection of Immortality*, 69.

are not bound even by reason, then even this doesn't guarantee that all will ultimately come to God. Again, we will return to this point later in this chapter.

Finally, there is another significant problem with McLeod-Harrison's Master Argument. Why assume *without qualification* that "the permanent cessation of a human is a metaphysically bad event that undermines the divine nature"? Even granting his reasoning about structural values, this doesn't preclude the possibility that these values may be overridden, such as by considerations of justice in response to extreme human wickedness, which conceivably warrants the complete annihilation of certain human beings.[13] If human wickedness is itself a horrific offense against God, then wouldn't the persistence of rebellion for all eternity "undermine the divine nature"? The only way to avoid this "metaphysically bad" state of affairs is for the damned to be annihilated or for all persons to be saved. Next we will consider some philosophical reasons why the latter route is unacceptable.

PHILOSOPHICAL PROBLEMS WITH UNIVERSALISM

In the first chapter we noted numerous biblical problems with universalism. There are also significant philosophical difficulties with the view. In this section I will identify three of these. I will also discuss two other philosophical objections that have been pressed by some critics of universalism but which ultimately fail to undercut the view.

The Undermining of Salvation

One problem with universalism concerns an implication it has for the concept of salvation. If there is a fundamental theological claim about which all Christians should agree it is that the atoning work of Christ is effective to save sinners. And this salvation involves, at the least, preventing or rescuing people from the condemnation in hell that they deserve because of their moral rebellion against God. Now, according to universalists no one will ultimately be lost and separated from God forever. Some universalists

---

13. Or, depending upon the brand of conditionalism—specifically whether or not one sees annihilation of the soul as punitive—human wickedness might not be regarded as punishment so much as disqualifying certain humans from receiving the gift of everlasting life.

regard this as a *contingent* fact based on God's merciful choice to reconcile all people to himself. For instance, Hans Küng asserts that the New Testament teaches "the consummation of a salvation of all, an all-embracing mercy," though he acknowledges "the absolutely final possibility of distance from God, which man cannot of himself *a priori* exclude."[14] Other universalists maintain that the salvation of all can indeed be known *a priori*, and they are confident of this because they believe that given God's nature as a perfectly loving and omnipotent being, it is *necessarily* the case that he will ultimately restore everyone.[15] Thus, Thomas Talbott claims that "if God is a necessary being and omnipotence, omniscience, and loving kindness are among his essential properties," then the notion that some people will be separated from God forever "is not even possibly true."[16] Still others grant only the barest possibility that some will be lost forever. For example, Eric Reitan says, "it is possible for someone to freely reject God *forever*. But the possible world in which this occurs is so remote that there seems to be no good reason to think that it is actual."[17]

Despite the differences between these approaches in terms of the modal qualifiers of their theses, all of them affirm a strong epistemic *confidence* in the claim that everyone will be restored to God. So although they differ regarding their claims about the metaphysical possibility of ultimately lost souls, they all seem to agree that it is not a *practical* possibility that some will be lost forever. Now here is the problem. Normally, when we think of someone being "saved" from an unpleasant fate of some sort we think of that fate as having been a genuine possibility. Suppose someone prevents me from drinking a milk shake that has been poisoned. It would make sense to say that she "saved" me from becoming gravely ill or even dying. But if I find out later that there was no poison in the milk shake after all, then it would make no sense to say that the person really saved me from that fate. Similarly, if there is no hell or potential afterlife of suffering for the damned, then it makes little sense to say that Christ "saves" anyone. And if some do experience hell temporarily but it is guaranteed that everyone will be saved in the end, spared from annihilation or endless torment in hell, then the meaning of that salvation is undermined because it was never a

---

14. Küng, *Eternal Life?* 141–42.

15. Jonathan Kvanvig dubs these two universalist positions "contingent universalism" and "necessary universalism." See Kvanvig, *Problem of Hell*, 74–78.

16. Talbott, "Providence, Freedom, and Human Destiny," 227.

17. Reitan, "Human Freedom," 140 (emphasis in original).

real possibility that the damned could be annihilated or suffer endlessly.[18] Yes, they were saved from *more* suffering in hell, which is certainly a good thing. But they were not saved from ultimate extinction of the self or endless torment, which would be far greater. And since on the conditionalist and traditionalist views the actual losses of the damned are so much more extreme, the salvation of those who are redeemed is incomparably greater than it could ever be for the redeemed on the universalist view.

With regard to the strong, necessitarian view of universalism, the point can be made as follows. If God's loving and gracious nature is such that he would never allow anyone to be forever lost, then there is no possible world in which someone is not finally saved. But if in all possible worlds everyone is saved, then exactly what did Christ's atoning work *save* us from? Granted, the universalist may still affirm the effectiveness of the atonement to achieve the propitiation of sins, the restoration of harmonious fellowship with God, and even from the temporary torments of hell. But the universalist cannot say that Christ's work saved us from permanent separation from God. So on the universalist view, the gift of salvation is not nearly so precious and profound as on the traditionalist and conditionalist accounts. And to the extent that salvation *appears* to be as significant for the universalist as on these non-universalist views, it is merely an illusion.[19]

Here the Calvinist universalist may object that when it comes to the elect, their fate is never in doubt anyway. God predestined his church from the foundation of the world to dwell with him for all eternity, so it was not really possible for them to be condemned. Their heavenly fate was always sealed. This is no more true for the elect on the universalist view than it is on the traditionalist and conditionalist views. Therefore, it is inappropriate to say that the universalist concept of salvation is less substantial. In response, I would note that, with some tweaking, this argument may still work against the Calvinist universalist, as follows. Granted, given Calvinism, it is never possible, per divine decree, for the elect to perish or suffer in hell eternally. And this is so on any of the three views of hell. However, on the traditionalist and conditionalist views, it is the case that for any particular elect person, he or she *could* have been rejected by God and abandoned to his or her sins and, ultimately, condemnation in hell. In other words, for any given elect person, there is a counter-factual possibility that they could

---

18. Robert L. Dabney presents a crude version of this argument in his *Lectures in Systematic Theology*, 857.

19. I have Chris Mullen to thank for this version of my argument.

have been among the non-elect and ended up in hell rather than in heaven. But this is not the case with universalism, where there is no such counterfactual possibility for any of the elect because everyone in the end is saved. So even for the non-universalist Calvinist there is a significant sense in which the elect are saved from a horrible possible fate. Not so for the universalist. Therefore, it appears that the concept of salvation is diminished given universalism, regardless of whether one is an Arminian or Calvinist.

Now even if the above problems could be evaded by the universalist, it should be noted that there remains an argument against universalism here which is *comparative* in nature. That is, when compared to the traditionalist and conditionalist views, there is a diminished concept of salvation on the universalist view. Or, to put it positively, the traditionalist and conditionalist views offer a much more substantial concept of salvation. This is because for the traditionalist and conditionalist, the alternative fate of damnation is *real* for many people, not just a perceived or logical possibility. On these views the redeemed are spared horrific fates which some fellow humans actually suffer. Not so for universalism, where God ensures that everyone is spared. So the meaning of salvation for the traditionalist and conditionalist is far more robust and significant than on the universalist view.

The Gratuity of Earthly Existence

Michael Murray has argued that universalism suffers from a problem of gratuitous evil in the sense that it "admits instances of evil which cannot be justified as in some sense a necessary condition for the occurrence of some greater good or prevention of some greater evil."[20] The evils to which Murray refers are all of the evils one experiences during one's earthly sojourn, presumably including pains and sorrows as well as indulgences in immorality. The problem is that, given the universalist thesis that everyone winds up in a state of perfect fellowship with God, no one's ultimate salvation is contingent upon choices they make during their earthly lifetime. So all of the evils they experience are utterly unnecessary. Murray asks,

> Why would God prefer to have us spend our first seventy or so years of existence in this earthly phase, enjoying a measure of intrinsic good but with the accompanying evil required to secure it, rather than positioning us in such a way that these years are spent in perfect communion with Him in Heaven? After all, any

20. Murray, "Three Versions," 56.

earthly goods obtained would pale in comparison with the goods achieved by spending those years in this way.[21]

A problem with Murray's argument is his assumption that all of the goods achieved during one's earthly phase will necessarily "pale in comparison" to the goods we might have achieved during the same timespan in heaven. Here the Hickian soul-making theodicist will insist that this is not necessarily the case. After all, such character traits as patience, mercy, forgiveness, courage, and perseverance may be developed in our current fallen state but are impossible to develop in a heavenly condition where there are no evils with which to contend. So although it is true, on the universalist account, that no human choices on earth could possibly preclude our ultimate arrival in heaven and an eternity of perfect communion with God, our choices do make a difference with regard to the shape of our moral characters which we take to the next world. So it appears that Murray's criticism focuses too narrowly upon the universalist thesis that all are saved without paying due attention to the *quality* of the individual souls who are saved.

Murray actually addresses this objection and grants that it has some merit. But he raises a counter-objection which he considers devastating to the soul-making approach. While the prospect of cultivating strong moral character is a worthy end that might justify the means of experiences of evil in this world for those who make the right choices along the way, Murray asks,

> What of those who failed to do so? Either they will be "miraculously transformed" into lovers of God, or they will spend eternity in the presence of God, but be unable to enjoy it. If the former, then the evil *in via* is thoroughly gratuitous. But if it is the latter, then there are some for whom existence in heaven will be tantamount to a life in hell. Those who have cultivated self-loving characters will not find happiness in being forced to commune with God and so will despise their existence.[22]

With this dilemma Murray rests his case regarding the universalist's problem of gratuitous evil. But has he really pinned the universalist with this argument? Murray assumes that when it comes to the morally recalcitrant who do not positively develop their characters on earth, the universalist must admit that they are miraculously, presumably instantaneously,

---

21. Ibid., 57.
22. Ibid., 58.

transformed into fully virtuous people, otherwise they would never enjoy their heavenly existence. But why suppose the transformation must be miraculously instantaneous? A more sophisticated universalism, which Murray himself discusses but fails to apply to this particular problem, says that the morally obstinate on earth may be gradually transformed through life in another environment, a post-mortem state where they eventually make choices that result in the proper soul-cultivation to prepare them for heaven. In this way, God could ensure that no one experiences truly gratuitous evil, even if their initial earthly phase was a "waste," so to speak. For all we know, some people's personalities are so constituted that they require a much longer travail than most in order to be effectively prompted to make their way to a well-ordered character. This might even be true for *most* people. Yet this doesn't mean that their experiences on earth were wasted. As Robin Parry points out, "that the majority of people do not embrace salvation in this life does not mean that their experiences now do not lay a foundation for a later acceptance of it. It could well be that without the experiences in this life salvation would take much longer to be attained in the post-mortem state."[23] The sort of "foundation" to which Parry refers here might include the natural and moral evils themselves that Murray wants to declare gratuitous. The impact of such evils on a person, however obdurate in this life, could conceivably have a cumulative effect such that by the time of the post-mortem state she is far more inclined to see her own depravity and need for redemption and thus more prepared to surrender to God. Of course, this is speculative, but it's very plausibility is sufficient to rebut Murray's objection, which aims to show that universalism implies gratuitous evil on earth.

Restricting Human Freedom

If Murray's argument from gratuitous evil ultimately misses its mark, it is nonetheless useful in prompting us to consider a distinct but related problem for universalism, and that is the supposed *guarantee* that all will be saved. For those universalists who espouse a libertarian conception of human freedom, this creates a major tension. First, let's recall exactly what libertarianism entails. The standard conception is that libertarian free will involves the *power of contrary choice*. That is, "I freely chose X" means that at the moment of choosing X, even if all of the conditions that obtained at

---

23. MacDonald (Parry), *Evangelical Universalist*, 162.

Hell, Immortality, and Salvation

the moment of my choosing were the same, I could have made a choice contrary to X. And that is to say, in order for my choice to be free in any instance, nothing can *guarantee* that I make a particular choice.

Let's apply this to the universalist claim that everyone will be saved. If the universalist believes that certain human choices are necessary conditions for personal salvation (e.g., the choice to accept God's grace) and such choices must be free in the libertarian sense, then there can be no guarantee that everyone will be saved. For such a guarantee is inconsistent with libertarian free will, as we just saw. The only way that it can be guaranteed in advance that everyone will be saved is if it is also guaranteed in advance that everyone will make the choice to turn to God, and this is not possible if human beings always have the power of contrary choice. So it seems the universalist must either surrender libertarian free will or else give up the guarantee that all will be saved, which is also to surrender confidence in universalism.[24]

In view of this difficulty, the universalist might try to steer between the horns of the dilemma by noting that God does respect our freedom but graciously refuses to allow the choices of some people to have their full effect when it comes to final human destiny. It is, after all, God's prerogative to miraculously change anyone he wants into a virtue-seeking, God-loving person once they arrive in the eschaton. Even if someone lived a thoroughly vicious life, God may, out of his merciful love, redeem them anyway. In this way, the freedom of the wicked person is respected, since God permitted them to make wrong choices throughout their life, but his transforming grace is applied in the afterlife in such a way that they will have a new, virtuous, God-loving character. Now the problem with this approach is that it ignores a critical feature of human freedom, which is that our choices have consequences in the real world. In my dream states, I make all sorts of choices. But my freedom in that imagined realm is not significant because those choices do not have consequences in reality. Similarly, on the universalist approach just described, the wicked person who is miraculously transformed is not truly free because this transformation is in no way connected with any choices she has made. In fact, the transformation *contradicts* her life's pattern of choices. This seems to be anything but a respect for human freedom. Michael Murray presents this analogy:

> On the picture proposed by the universalist, it is as if one were to go to the drive-through window at a fast food restaurant, make a

---

24. For another version of this argument, see Kvanvig, *Problem of Hell*, 77–78.

selection, and order. But, no matter what is ordered, the attendant hands over the same food. If you order fish, you get a hamburger, if you order ice cream, you get a hamburger, if you order french fries, you get a hamburger.... You are welcome to freely choose whatever menu item you like, but at this restaurant, you have it *their* way. And so it is on the universalist picture. You are welcome to do whatever you like, but with God, you have it *His* way. As a result, while free choosing may go on in the universalist's world, it is a free choosing that is without autonomy, since one is transformed into a lover of God, whether one chooses to be such or not.[25]

Murray goes on to note a possible line of response from the universalist, which would be to say that a divinely imposed limitation on autonomy is well worth it, if it means the avoidance of eternal separation from God.[26] After all, the consequences of evil earthly choices are so much more severe in the eschaton. The problem with this reply, he points out, is that it overlooks the fact that the consequences of evil earthly choices are actually far *more* severe on earth where our free actions often hurt other people. Thus, Murray concludes, "since limited autonomy is not found in the earthly arena, we have no reason to think that different principles would be at work in the case of eternity."[27]

Some universalists are likely to respond to this by insisting that people are not changed into God-lovers through instantaneous miraculous transformation but through something more subtle, what we might call divine interference. Eric Reitan, for example, proposes that if a person's obstinate resistance to divine grace is due to their ignorance or bondage to desire, then it is appropriate for God to intervene in such a way as to remove this hindrance to redemption. After all, their ignorance or bondage to desire are not enabling their libertarian freedom but actually restricting it. Therefore, Reitan contends, "God would not be violating human freedom by eliminating such ignorance or bondage to desire."[28] So why should anyone complain that God intervenes, even sometimes dramatically, to turn the most recalcitrant sinners to himself? However, such a response undermines the univer-

---

25. Murray, "Three Versions," 59.

26. MacDonald (Parry) takes such an approach, suggesting that "if all else fails, [God] would be justified in not leaving people free in a libertarian sense with respect to their salvation. This is preferable to allowing them to suffer in everlasting conscious torment" (*Evangelical Universalist*, 23).

27. Murray, "Three Versions," 60.

28. Reitan, "Human Freedom," 133.

Hell, Immortality, and Salvation

salist position. Here is why. Either God's interference to save the obstinate is resistible or it is not. If it is resistible, then there is no guarantee that God will save everyone in the end, as some may freely resist his efforts, in which case the universalist cannot be confident that everyone will be saved. But if God's efforts are *not* resistible, then those who come to him as a result do not do so freely and therefore cannot be said to truly desire God's grace and salvation. On what basis, then, should God grant them salvation? If a person can be saved without ever freely choosing to accept his grace, then why should God have ever bothered giving human beings libertarian freedom?

Thomas Talbott counters this argument by suggesting that it is possible for even a libertarian free will to infallibly choose rightly, and all this requires is that the person be "fully informed" about what is best for them and an absence of impediments to the choice of that good. Talbott says, "once all ignorance and deception and bondage to desire is removed, so that a person is truly 'free' to choose, there can no longer be any motive for choosing eternal misery for oneself."[29] There are several problems with Talbott's argument. First, his claim contradicts the common phenomenon of moral weakness, where a person knows that X is the best or right choice and yet chooses not-X. While one of the great mysteries of human psychology, moral weakness is a widely recognized fact about human nature regarding which many philosophers and psychologists have puzzled, going all the way back to Aristotle.[30] Second, Reitan assumes a controversial view of the relation between human will and cognition, which sees the two as easily disentangled such that the latter can be thoroughly informed and "cleansed" of malignant influences and significant interference from the will. In fact, one of the major lessons of the history of science, highlighted in the last few decades of philosophy of science, is that even the most informed and rigorous empirical scientists are subject to unwitting distortion of the facts due to their unreflective biases and prejudices.[31] And, thirdly, we might even appeal to the story of Adam and Eve in Genesis 2–3. They suffered no significant ignorance about their good. They were informed of the consequences of eating from the tree of the knowledge of good and evil—that if they did so, they would "certainly die" (Gen 2:17). And, as yet

---

29. Talbott, "Everlasting Punishment," 37.

30. See Aristotle, *Nicomachean Ethics*, book VII. For some good contemporary discussions of moral weakness, see Davidson, "How Is Weakness," 93–113; Lukes, "Moral Weakness," 104–14; and Mortimore, *Weakness of Will*.

31. I borrow this line of criticism from Kvanvig, *The Problem of Hell*, 79–80.

Hell and Divine Goodness

unfallen and morally pure human beings, they suffered from no bondage to desire. Yet, they both chose wrongly. Admittedly, Eve was deceived by the serpent, but Adam was not deceived (cf. 1 Tim 2:14), yet he chose wrongly anyway in what is perhaps a paradigm case of moral weakness. All of these considerations show Talbott's "full information" approach to be seriously flawed.

A potential way out for the universalist here is simply to embrace compatibilism. I know of no universalist who does so in a thoroughgoing way. But, whether or not there are any compatibilist universalists, we may ask whether this is a *reasonable* option. Perhaps not, since, as just noted, it might undermine the genuineness of the divine-human relationship. If compatibilism is true, then God is free to determine human wills any way he wants, and this includes decreeing pure continuous hate and vice in the hearts and minds of the damned such that there is literally nothing good in them worth saving. Moreover, if compatibilism is true, God *could* make certain people perfectly unredeemable in the sense that their natures are so twisted that they become virtually identical with their vices.[32] Thus, in a sense, they are perfectly fit for nothing else but their hellish existence. Perhaps Satan and his demonic horde would fit this description, as might certain human beings who are sufficiently morally degenerated. But if all of this is *possible*, and it seems to be given compatibilism, then this in turn undermines the standard universalist assumption that God *necessarily* wants everyone to be saved. For the preservation of such extreme and determinedly unrepentant persons might contradict divine goodness and thus reasonably motivate God to remove them from his presence forever or, what I believe would be best, annihilate them. Now if all of this is possible given a compatibilist view of freedom, then the universalist, again, loses her basis for confidence that God will save everyone. So the compatibilist option doesn't help the situation for the universalist.

---

32. C. S. Lewis describes some people in this way. To those who refuse to repent of, say, grumbling, he says "[You] can repent and come out of it again. But there may come a day when you can do that no longer. Then there will be no *you* left to criticize the mood, nor even to enjoy it but just the grumble itself going on forever like a machine" (*The Great Divorce*, 75).

Restricting Divine Freedom

As we've seen, the difficulty that universalism creates regarding human freedom has been much discussed. A less well-known problematic implication of universalism pertains to a challenge it presents for *divine* freedom. In brief, to say that God must preserve all people for all eternity is to imply that there are significant limits on the freedom of God. Paul Helm has claimed that God no more must love everyone equally than he must create them with equal characteristics. In addressing the common universalist argument that God's love and justice dictate that he will ultimately redeem all people, Helm notes that this "carries the absurd consequence for any theist who takes the idea of divine creation seriously, that God could not have created a universe in which people were significantly different from each other, or in which anything was significantly different from anything else." He goes on to say that such a view implies that "while God can be arbitrary or particular with regard to, say, sex, hair-colour, and I.Q., he cannot be arbitrary or particular over any person's eternal salvation."[33]

The universalist's likely reply is that God is free to make people significantly different from one another, but his equal and maximal love for all people simply guarantees that he will preserve all of them forever. However, the notion that God loves all people equally has been subjected to some serious challenges. Thomas Aquinas saw God's varying degrees of love for different things as following from the fact that God wills different purposes for different things. As he expressed it, "God's loving one thing more than another is nothing else than His willing for that thing a greater good."[34] And it is clear from the context that Aquinas maintained that God's love for humans in particular varies.

Recently, Jeff Jordan has developed a more sophisticated objection to the notion that God's love must be maximally extended and equally intense (LME). Jordan proceeds using a perfect being theology which affirms that God possesses every great-making property. Universalists typically take this approach in defense of their thesis that God saves everyone: Since God is perfectly loving, he must love everyone according to LME, therefore everyone will be saved. However, the trouble for the universalist is that, despite initial appearances, LME is not truly a great-making quality. To show this, Jordan begins with the assumption that any quality which would be a

---

33. Helm, "Logic of Limited Atonement," 54.
34. Aquinas, *Summa Theologica*, 116.

defect or deficiency in a human being cannot be a great-making quality in a perfect being and thus cannot be an attribute of God. And loving all people with equal intensity would surely be a defect in a human being. Jordan explains why:

> a human who loved all other humans equally and impartially would have a life significantly impoverished. Much of the richness of life flows from one's friendships and one's spouse and one's children, and within these attachments there is a love which is neither impartial nor equally shared by all other persons, as one loves her beloved more than she does others. It is not just that one manifests her love for the beloved differently from how one manifests her love for others. No, a person appropriately loves his own children more than other children. And without the inequality of love, one's life would be diminished. . . . Indeed, a life in which all loves are flat . . . is clearly a defective life.[35]

Jordan's point, then, is that since LME would be a vice in human beings, it cannot be a virtue, much less a great-making quality, in the deity. So God must not have the property of LME. Thomas Talbott has critiqued Jordan's argument on the grounds that it ignores the vastly different capacities possessed by God and human beings, which explains why LME would be a defect in humans but it is nonetheless a divine perfection. He notes that "our normal human limitations typically detract from the quality of our deepest attachments," but, in contrast, "God has none of the human limitations that make it impossible for us to achieve an equally intimate relationship with all created persons during our earthly lives."[36]

Talbott's critique is apposite and might in fact succeed in defeating Jordan's argument. Still, Talbott fails to demonstrate that LME is a divine property. He has only refuted—if he has done that—Jordan's critique of the notion that LME is a divine property. There remains the problem of freedom as it relates to the matter of divine love. To insist that God loves all people with equal intensity implies that God is not free to will significantly different purposes. For the universalist, then, LME inhibits divine creative freedom in several crucial respects. First, it would limit God *ontologically*. God could only will different purposes for people within the parameters of keeping them all alive forever. That is, he would be constrained not to create any temporary people. Any human creation is an eternal commitment for

---

35. Jordan, "Topography," 60–61.
36. Talbott, "Topography," 309, 311.

God, given LME. Secondly, LME would limit God *morally*. God could only make people who would eventually submit to him in faith and repentance. Thus, God's creative freedom would be limited to creating people with certain limitations of freedom of their own. And, finally, LME would limit God *aesthetically*. God could only instantiate a world with a limited range of ultimate drama, such that there are no extreme contrasts of destiny between the virtuous and the wicked. Yes, there could still be heaven and hell, but since the latter is only a temporary phase on some people's journey to heaven, the drama is not nearly so rich as that in which ultimate separation from God is an actual destiny for some people.

These are significant constraints on God and his freedom to create. Now the universalist may attempt to justify this in terms of some ultimate value constraints dictated by God's own aims and desires. One possible value constraint is utilitarian in nature—the good of maximizing happiness. One might argue that a perfect being would want to make a universe in which there is maximal pleasure and joy. But even granting the questionable notion that God is a cosmic hedonist, why think that preserving *all* people for eternity will necessarily result in maximum happiness? Definitely such a value constraint rules out traditionalism, since ECT guarantees untold misery for all eternity. And whatever else one thinks might obtain in a maximally happy world, surely the existence of people suffering eternal torment would be ruled out. So, then, what of conditionalism? For the damned, on this view, all misery eventually ceases. Of course, there is the problem of heavenly grief—the sorrows that could plague the blessed in heaven as they contemplate the fate of their damned loved ones and friends. This is a significant issue, and we will deal with it at length in the next chapter where I will suggest a way in which the conditionalist (and traditionalist, for that matter) might avoid any grieving of the damned in hell.

Another potential value constraint on God's freedom to create is aesthetic in nature, namely the constraint to maximize beauty. Thus, the universalist could argue that God's preserving all people eternally will ultimately make for the most beautiful story. And if a perfect being would want to make the most beautiful story of humanity, then God would ensure that all people live forever in blessed union with him. But, again, why believe that the universalist story is the most beautiful one? While many people may regard this as the most pleasing story in certain respects, a story in which some, if only a comparatively small number, are lost forever might be more beautiful overall because of the "higher stakes" of the drama and the consequent greater intensity of the gratitude for grace and mercy that this would produce among those who are saved.

So it is not clear how the universalist could justify the strong limitations—ontological, moral, and aesthetic—on God's freedom to create which are implied by the LME requirement regarding God's love. It appears, then, that the universalist faces a severe problem when it comes to the matter of divine freedom.

Dabney's Wager

A final argument which warrants mention originates from the nineteenth-century Presbyterian theologian Robert Dabney. It takes the form of a Pascal-style argument from prudence rather than from evidence. As Dabney presents it, "whether universalism be true or false, it is absurdity to teach it. If it turns out true, no one will have lost his soul for not learning it. If it turns out false, everyone who has embraced it thereby will incur an immense and irreparable evil. Hence, though the probabilities of its truth were as a million to one, it would be madness and cruelty to teach it."[37] Thus, the point of the argument is that there is nothing to gain and terribly much to lose by endorsing universalism. So it is folly to teach the view. Now, as stated, Dabney's argument is obviously problematic insofar as he apparently assumes that everyone who affirms universalism is destined for hell. But, of course, there is no reason to believe this. Presumably, universalism does not constitute the unforgiveable sin of Mark 3:29. Whatever negative repercussions await any of us for holding an incorrect view on hell, so long as we are in Christ, we will still be saved from hell.

More recently, critics of universalism have presented the objection in a way that is specifically focused on the supposed detrimental effect that universalism might have regarding evangelism. J. I. Packer warns that "universalist speculation . . . is a very great evil, calculated to blight a ministry." After all, he argues, if we believe everyone will be saved in the end, then "the decisiveness of decisions made in this life, and the urgency of evangelism here in this life, immediately, are undermined."[38] A similar argument has been made by Jay Wesley Richards, who argues that if universalism were widely embraced, missionary activity and evangelism "would surely be less common, since its urgency would be diminished. After all, what mission-

37. Dabney, *Systematic Theology*, 861.
38. Packer, "Problem of Universalism," 178, 171.

Hell, Immortality, and Salvation

ary would be willing to die in his or her own pool of blood at the hands of pagan tribes if the salvation of such tribes were in no way dependent on such risk?"[39]

In light of these points from Packer and Richards, then, we may revise Dabney's original argument as follows:

1. If universalism is true then teaching the doctrine provides no benefits, since everyone will be saved in the end anyway.
2. If universalism is false then teaching the doctrine will cause serious harm, since the urgency of turning to Christ for salvation will be undermined and more people than otherwise will end up in hell.
3. Therefore, there are great potential costs and no significant benefits to teaching universalism.
4. Therefore, it is imprudent to teach universalism.

This version of the argument is stronger than Dabney's but is nonetheless still problematic. For one thing, the universalist will be quick to point out, there are also potential costs to teaching non-universalist doctrines of hell, especially the traditional doctrine of ECT, which is a major stumbling block for many and a favorite argument against theism. Atheist and Christian scholars alike have argued that the problem of hell is the worst aspect of the problem of evil for Christians,[40] and common experience confirms this as religious skeptics frequently cite the (traditional) doctrine of hell among their reasons for rejecting Christianity. So if teaching universalism is problematic because it undermines the urgency to surrender to God, then teaching the traditionalist doctrine of ECT might be just as problematic because it undermines our concept of the love and mercy of God. Furthermore, the universalist might add, concerns about undermining the urgency of repentance associated with teaching universalism might be offset by the attractiveness of the higher degree of hope and encouragement that universalism provides for many of its proponents.

Some further points can be made in defense of universalism with regard to the charge that it undermines the motivation for evangelism and missionary work. First, the Christian's primary motive for such outreach is not prevention of damnation but simple obedience to the charge of Christ

---

39. Richards, "Pascalian Argument," 216.
40. See, respectively, Lewis, "Divine Evil" and Adams, "The Problem of Hell."

to "make disciples of all nations... teaching them to obey everything I have commanded you" (Matt 28:19–20). This "Great Commission" mandate provides all the incentive that Christians should need to preach and teach the gospel to the lost. Furthermore, assuming that the version of universalism we are considering is of the restorationist variety, which affirms the reality of hell, Christian universalists *do* have the additional evangelistic motivation to prevent people from going to hell. If restorationist universalism is true, then, for all we know, people might suffer in hell for a long period of time, perhaps years or even centuries, before finally being redeemed. So what reasonable missionary would not be willing to put his or her life on the line to prevent such horrible torment? Why must the prospect of everlasting torment or annihilation be necessary to properly motivate Christians to do such sacrificial work? It is like thinking that a physician has no motive to treat a patient for any illness that is not life-threatening or supposing that a defense attorney only has an adequate incentive to defend clients who are accused of capital crimes. Such logic defies common sense.[41]

We may conclude, then, that Dabney's wager, though interesting and worthy of consideration, ultimately fails to demonstrate that it is foolish to defend or teach universalism. Although, as we've seen, universalism is deeply problematic, worries about the potential practical consequences of teaching universalism are not reasonable grounds for its rejection.

ON SECOND CHANCES AND ESCAPING HELL

We have noted several good philosophical reasons for rejecting the doctrine of universalism. That is, we are warranted in believing that not everyone is saved in the end. At least some people are eternally separated from God. And given the severe problems with the traditionalist doctrine of eternal conscious torment, this constitutes a fairly strong recommendation of the conditionalist view. It is important to note, however, that rejection of universalism does not entail that we must reject the possibility of escape from hell. That is, although restorationism might be false as a *universal* thesis, non-universalist views are nevertheless consistent with the claim that some people ultimately escape hell and are restored to God. For non-Calvinists, especially, the possibility of some sort of post-mortem "second chance,"

---

41. For a good discussion of these and other points, see MacDonald (Robin Parry), *Evangelical Universalist*, 168–72 and John Kronen and Eric Reitan, *God's Final* Victory, 183–84.

whether truly the possibility of escaping hell or just an opportunity to accept saving grace in an interim state, is attractive. After all, if God loves everyone and wants all people to be saved, then it seems unfair and undesirable that during their earthly sojourns some people are given far more opportunities for grace than other people. John Wesley expressed serious anxiety over this: "Why is it . . . that so vast a majority of mankind are, so far as we can judge, cut off from all means, all possibility of holiness, even from their mother's womb? For instance: what possibility is there that a Hottentot, a New Zealander, or an inhabitant of Nova-Zembla, if he lives and dies there, should ever know what holiness means? Or, consequently, ever attain it?"[42] While Wesley himself never arrived at a satisfactory answer to his questions, some have appealed to the possibility of escape from hell as a solution. For example, Andrei Buckareff and Allen Plug argue that since God maintains an "open door" policy in accepting the penitent in this world, it would be out of character for God to cut off all opportunity for reconciliation in the next world. They write,

> God's desire for a restored relationship with us, His estranged children, should lead God to adopt policies in the eschaton that would reflect such a desire and other pro-attitudes. God's soteriological policies would be entirely disharmonious with what appear to be God's policies this side of the eschaton if God's policies change in the afterlife to include a "closed-door" policy towards His creatures that bear God's image.[43]

For this reason, Buckareff and Plug maintain, opportunities for forgiveness and redemption must extend even beyond the grave, and this means "the possibility of escape from hell must always be there for the residents of hell."[44] Jerry Walls offers a different sort of argument for the escapist view, appealing to what he calls "optimal grace," where God ensures that every person is afforded adequate opportunities to receive salvation. With certain qualifications, Walls suggests that God distributes his grace equally to all in the sense that an "optimal measure is given to all persons and all are given full opportunity to make a decisive response to it, either positively or negatively."[45] For Walls such optimal grace entails something like purgatory

---

42. Wesley, "Imperfection," 582.
43. Buckareff and Plug, "Escaping Hell," 44.
44. Ibid.
45. Walls, *Hell*, 89.

or an interim post-mortem state that affords further opportunities to submit to God.

So, like Buckareff and Plug, Walls maintains that there is hope for redemption for the impenitent in the afterlife. Their arguments and views differ in a variety of ways, however. Walls' argument is grounded in the concept of fairness, while that of Buckareff and Plug reasons from divine moral consistency. Also, Walls doesn't go so far as to suggest, as Buckareff and Plug do, that the possibility of reconciliation is "always" there for those in hell. Nor does Walls seem willing to grant that people may be literally saved out of hell, though he grants the possibility of redemption in a post-mortem, perhaps purgatorial, interim state. This raises the question regarding the relationship between hell and purgatory, regarding which there is a variety of perspectives, including the view that purgatory and hell are actually the same thing.[46]

What are we to say regarding the idea of post-mortem conversion? There are potential difficulties with the view. Returning to a problem discussed above, might such opportunities for salvation undermine the urgency of turning to God and obeying him, thus cheapening grace? Both Walls and Buckareff and Plug address this problem. The latter emphasize the importance of submitting to God in this world in order to be better prepared for our heavenly state: "Waiting only postpones the process in question, making it more difficult for us to be fit for communion with God due to persistent recalcitrance and obduracy."[47] Similarly, Walls replies that complacency here on earth which involves putting off accepting God's grace will only create a pattern of rejection that could eventually ensure that a person continues to do so in the next world. So it would never be in a person's interest to procrastinate their repentance and turning to God.[48]

---

46. C. S. Lewis poses the question whether there is a way out of hell, and his answer is as follows:

> It depends on the way ye're using the words. If they leave that grey town behind it will not have been Hell. To any that leaves it, it is Purgatory. And perhaps ye had better not call this country Heaven. Not Deep Heaven, ye understand.... Ye can call it the Valley of the Shadow of Life. And yet to those who stay here it will have been Heaven from the first. And ye can call those sad streets in the town yonder the Valley of the Shadow of Death: but to those who remain there they will have been Hell even from the beginning.
>
> (*The Great Divorce*, 67)

47. Buckareff and Plug, "Escaping Hell," 52.

48. Walls puts it like this: "If such persons continue to reject salvation on the presumption that they can repent later, it may well be that they are forming, by that very

Hell, Immortality, and Salvation

Walls also raises the problem of evangelism much like that facing the universalist which was discussed above. If we could be confident that God will ensure that everyone is ultimately given an equal shot at redemption, then why extend considerable efforts reaching people with the gospel in distant lands? Walls replies that we should be no less motivated to help people find salvation in this world because of the sheer joy of seeing them redeemed.[49] Here one could also appeal, as noted above, to the Great Commission mandate as sufficient motive to evangelize. The command of Christ to spread the gospel should put to rest once and for all any practical concerns about missionary incentive. Anyone who demands stronger motivation is simply making excuses.

Walls' and Buckareff and Plug's concepts of post-mortem opportunities for salvation provide a helpful nuance for non-Calvinist traditionalist and conditionalist views of hell. In addition to accounting for divine moral consistency and an ultimately fair system of opportunities for salvation, it also precludes any possibility that a person could be blameworthy, if only in part, for the damnation of someone else. If X fails, whether out of laziness or incompetence, to effectively present the gospel to Y, then this could make the difference between Y's finding redemption and eternal life or being damned to eternal torment or annihilation. But if there are post-mortem opportunities for salvation, then this removes a psychologically unhealthy pressure to evangelize, not to mention feelings of guilt and shame which naturally accompany such pressure.

In any case, there appear to be good philosophical reasons to take seriously the claim that even after death a person may avert or even escape hell. Moreover, it seems that the traditionalist and the conditionalist may embrace such a view no less than the universalist. That is, there is nothing inherent to any of the three views that would contradict post-mortem second chances for the as-yet unsaved. It is just that the universalist alone insists that *all* of the denizens of hell will eventually find their way to salvation.

---

attitude, a settled disposition to prefer their will to God's. At the very least, this may make it much more difficult for them to come to accept God's will" (*Hell*, 94).

49. Walls effectively addresses numerous other objections to his proposal. See *Hell*, 93–102.

CONCLUSION

We began this chapter with a discussion of several arguments aimed at showing that human beings are naturally immortal, specifically arguments proposed by Socrates, Aquinas, and McLeod-Harrison. We found that all of these arguments fail. Next we discussed five different arguments against universalism. We found that two of these, Murray's argument from the gratuity of earthly suffering and Dabney's wager, can be effectively rebutted by the universalist. But three other arguments, from the nature of salvation, human freedom, and divine freedom, do present serious problems for universalism. Finally, we considered the prospect of post-mortem opportunities to be saved, whether in the context of an interim state or from hell itself, and we noted that there appear to be no good reasons to reject the possibility and some good reasons to affirm it, regardless of whether one is a traditionalist, conditionalist, or universalist.

5

Hell and Heavenly Bliss

We have already discussed several objections to the traditional doctrine of hell as eternal conscious torment. One of these concerns problems related to the appropriateness of the punishment itself, given the apparent injustice of punishing finite sins with everlasting torment, while another regards the problem of eternally persistent evil which ECT entails. Both of these problems challenge the traditional view on the basis of certain intuitions regarding the nature of God, specifically, the apparent incompatibility of ECT with God's goodness. A less frequently discussed problem related to the traditional view concerns the apparent incompatibility of ECT with another kind of goodness, namely the bliss of the redeemed in heaven. How, it may be asked, could I be truly happy in heaven, knowing that some of my loved ones are experiencing non-stop torment in hell? The question may be posed as a challenge to the conditionalist view as well: How can I experience true heavenly bliss if some of my loved ones are destroyed for all eternity, never to live again? In this chapter we will address this question, exploring some common responses as well as counter-replies, which in turn raise a cluster of complex psychological and moral issues.

THE PROBLEM OF HEAVENLY GRIEF

What I intend to focus on here regards a problem that hell's torments present for non-universalist views of hell—a difficulty that I will call *the problem of heavenly grief*. According to Christian theology, heaven is an ideal place

Hell and Divine Goodness

or condition where God wipes away every tear and there is no more pain or sorrow (cf. Rev 21:4). Yet knowledge of the suffering of the damned would seem to have a negative psychological impact on those in heaven, particularly the loved ones of the damned. Friedrich Schleiermacher expresses the problem as follows:

> If we . . . consider eternal damnation as it is related to eternal bliss, it is easy to see that once the former exists, the latter can exist no longer. Even if externally the two realms were quite separate, yet so high a degree of bliss is not as such compatible with entire ignorance of others' misery, the more so if the separation itself is the result purely of a general judgment, at which both sides were present, which means conscious each of the other. Now if we attribute to the blessed a knowledge of the state of the damned, it cannot be a knowledge unmixed with sympathy. If the perfecting of our nature is not to move backwards, sympathy must be such as to embrace the whole human race, and when extended to the damned must of necessity be a disturbing element in bliss, all the more that, unlike similar feelings in this life, it is untouched by hope. . . . Thus our sympathy cannot fail to be attended by the bitter feeling always present when we see a real connexion between our own gain and another's loss.[1]

Schleiermacher takes this problem to be devastating for the traditional view of hell and, for that matter, any other non-universalist view of hell. To get a clearer picture of the problem, it will help to do a comparative assessment of the three views of hell as pertains to this issue.

For the universalist, a grief-free awareness of the suffering of their loved ones in hell seems plausible, in that hell's torment may be regarded as the necessary means of prompting repentance and eventual joyful reunion in heaven. Thus, for the universalist, suffering in hell may be comparable to, say, an extremely redemptive prison term or even a lengthy surgical procedure on the soul, performed, as it were, without anesthesia. In either case, the imprisonment or surgery is guaranteed to work, and its benefits will be eternally blissful. In light of such a positive permanent outcome, the time during which loved ones are in hell need not cause any real grief for those concurrently in heaven.

---

1. Schleiermacher, *Christian Faith*, 721–22. For some recent variations of Schleiermacher's argument and careful discussion of critical responses, see Talbott, "Providence, Freedom, and Human Destiny," 237–41; Reitan, "Eternal Damnation," 429–50; and Kronen and Reitan, *God's Final Victory*, 80–89.

For the conditionalist, however, hell presents a real threat to heavenly bliss. For on this view the redeemed are not reunited with their loved ones. They are annihilated, never to be known again. It is difficult to imagine this not being a disturbing realization for the redeemed in heaven, for there is an extreme loss here—a permanently severed relationship. There is some consolation, however, vis-à-vis the traditional view, in at least two respects. First, the redeemed will know that their loved ones suffered just as long as they deserved, which, on the traditional view, is unintelligible, since everyone in hell suffers forever. Secondly, the redeemed will know that their loved ones are no longer suffering, nor will they ever suffer again.

For the traditionalist, however, the situation is much worse. Even if we assume for the moment that everlasting torment could somehow be just, the traditionalist must deal with the fact that for all eternity (at least many of) the redeemed in heaven will be aware that some of their loved ones are suffering unspeakable torments in hell. It is difficult to conceive how this awareness would not be disturbing, even realizing the perfect justice of the torment. Consider the following analogy. You are on an idyllic ocean cruise, enjoying the finest food, music, and fellowship possible with people who are wonderful in every way. But at the same time, you are aware that your mother, who had been invited to the same cruise, has been arrested for some horrible crime and is currently in solitary confinement. You know that she hates being alone, so the thought of her mental torture plagues you. And no matter how much your friends remind you that, well, she really brought it all on herself and deserves her suffering, this doesn't assuage your grief one iota. In fact, you feel ashamed to be enjoying yourself at all, given your mother's plight. Even though it is impossible for you to see her and offer her your comfort, you still find it difficult to enjoy the cruise. Indeed, the fact that you can't contact her despite her still being alive and conscious only adds to your anxiety and frustration.[2]

Now if your joy would be diminished by this knowledge of your mother's suffering in solitary confinement, albeit deserved, then how much more

---

2. This analogy, of course, has its limitations, but I think it captures some important dimensions of the contrast between the fates of the damned and the blessed in heaven which some other scholars' analogies fail to capture. For example, James Cain compares the situation to that of a person attending a party while his friend is "willfully and stubbornly sulking" at home. Cain insists that this would be a sad situation, but "recognizing something as a sad state of affairs need not make one sad" ("Existence of Heaven," 56). Implicitly comparing hell to a state of temporary stubborn sulking is very misleading, at least if we take seriously the biblical witness regarding the miserable condition of the damned.

so would the awareness of your mother being interminably tormented in hell disturb your peace of mind? Returning to the analogy, if your mother was finally executed, then, after a period of grieving, you would be able to eventually accept the finality of this and experience joy, since, after all, nothing could be done to bring her back and at least she's no longer suffering. This is analogous to the situation on the conditionalist view, which does mitigate the problem considerably, though difficulties do remain for the conditionalist.

As for the traditionalist, it seems the joy of personal redemption will be tainted for as long as one's loved ones are suffering in hell, which is forever. When we compare this outcome to that for the conditionalist, the contrast is potentially infinite, and here's why. For both the conditionalist and the traditionalist, there is utter hopelessness with regard to being reunited with one's damned loved one—in the former case because the loved one no longer exists and in the latter because it is divinely guaranteed that no one escapes from hell, at least on the standard traditional view. So the relevant difference between the two situations is that, after some relatively short period of time, the suffering stops for the damned in the former case, while it continues *eternally* in the latter case. So there is the potentially infinite difference.

ATTEMPTS AT A SOLUTION

Scholars have proposed a variety of approaches to solving the problem of heavenly grief. I will consider and assess several of these.

The Pleasing Justice Approach

One standard response to the problem of heavenly grief appeals to the perfect justice of the torment of the damned. We can trust that God will enable us to see how appropriate their fate is. We will so clearly perceive the justice of it, in fact, that we will actually be pleased by the prospect of their suffering. Peter Geach expresses this view of the matter when he declares, "someone confronted with the damned would find it impossible to wish that things so evil should be happy—particularly when the misery is seen as the direct and natural consequence of the guilt."[3] We may call

---

3. Geach, *Providence and Evil*, 139.

this line of reasoning the *pleasing justice* response. One problem with this approach is that it misses the point by addressing the wrong issue. It is one thing to be satisfied with a just punishment for a heinous crime. But such satisfaction does not preclude the possibility of deep grief over the broader situation that called for such punishment. Thus, Thomas Talbott critiques Geach's reasoning as follows: "From the premise that I could not wish to see my daughter both morally corrupt and happy, it simply does not follow that I would not wish to see her happy. Indeed, if my own daughter should become as corrupt and miserable as Geach describes, that would only increase the sense of loss and yearning for what could have been, the desire to see her both redeemed and happy."[4] So even perfect justice in hell is not a cure for grief over the suffering of the damned. Rather, it only restricts my regrets to the fact that my loved ones made choices such that this would be their just fate. This is more than enough to significantly tarnish one's heavenly condition.

Another difficulty with the pleasing justice response is the fact that it is questionable whether one could really be pleased by the suffering of the damned. After all, there is nothing analogous to this in our experience on earth. Rather, even for those who deserve to be imprisoned or executed, we take no pleasure in this. Though we may see the justice in it, we are disturbed by the prospect of the suffering itself. Even loved ones of murder victims typically don't find the executions or permanent incarcerations of the perpetrators to be pleasurable. Rather, they find satisfaction in the closure this brings, knowing the perpetrator is gone, never to be a threat again. Anyone who would actually take pleasure in the execution or incarceration would appear to us more likely as pathetic or psychologically disturbed, not enlightened or morally mature.

But with the traditional view of hell, we aren't talking about anything like execution or simple incarceration; we are talking about severe, unceasing *torment*. In earthly human experience, the idea that anyone would take pleasure in the suffering of others to any degree, let alone non-stop excruciating pain, is disturbing, to say the least. In fact, we would call such a person sadistic or psychologically sick, again, even if the suffering were fully deserved. So the notion that somehow in heaven we will be "miraculously changed" such that we can enjoy watching (or being constantly aware of) the intense suffering of other people seems tantamount to saying that God

---

4. Talbott, "Everlasting Punishment," 39.

will miraculously make us sadists. This hardly seems to be a satisfactory way of solving the problem of heavenly grief.

The Selective Amnesia Approach

An alternative way of dealing with the problem says that when you go to heaven God will have you forget your loved ones in hell. Since any memory of them would be accompanied by a sense of loss, even independently of the awareness of their torment, God can circumvent this problem by erasing all of your memories of them. William Lane Craig advocates such an approach when he says, "One could agree that knowledge of loved ones' damnation would undermine the supreme happiness of the redeemed, but maintain that it is possible that the redeemed in heaven have no such knowledge. Perhaps God obliterates from their minds any knowledge of lost persons so that they experience no pangs of remorse for them."[5] We might call this the *selective amnesia solution*. With the elimination of the memories of our lost loved ones, there remains no more basis for painful thoughts associated with them. This approach appears to be a moral improvement on the pleasing justice view. But does it work? One potential problem with this approach is that it assumes that heavenly blessedness is consistent with ignorance about some salient facts the knowledge of which would spoil that blessed state. Can one be said to be truly happy if someone they deeply love is in agony but they just aren't aware of this? Many would answer negatively, including Thomas Talbott who says a necessary condition for heavenly blessedness is that there are no facts such that if the person were aware of them their supreme happiness would be ruined. In other words, true heavenly blessedness must be "the kind of happiness that could survive a full disclosure of the facts."[6] Furthermore, says Talbott, for God to hide such facts from the redeemed would amount to an "immoral deception."

So Talbott essentially adjusts Schleiermacher's argument to qualify the conditions for eternal blessedness with the counterfactual claim that eternal blessedness is possible if and only if a person *would* remain in that blessed state even if they were to come to know all of the facts about the world.[7] Is Talbott's more stringent, counterfactual criterion for heavenly

5. Craig, "Talbott's Universalism," 306.
6. Talbott, "Providence, Freedom, and Human Destiny," 240.
7. For a helpful comparative analysis of Schleiermacher's and Talbott's arguments

bliss reasonable? It is hard to say. Craig is certainly unmoved by it, insisting that there is no reason to think it would be immoral of God to shield the redeemed from such painful knowledge. After all, says Craig, "We can all think of cases in which we shield persons from knowledge which would be painful for them and which they do not need to have, and, far from doing something immoral, we are, in so sparing them, exemplifying the virtue of mercy."[8] To this, Talbott retorts by citing cases where people ordinarily do *not* want to remain in ignorance of the fate of a loved one, "however painful the knowledge of such a fate might be."[9]

The debate between Talbott and Craig on this point seems inconclusive to me. Talbott's proposed counterfactual criterion for heavenly bliss has some intuitive plausibility, but he offers little evidential support for it. On the other hand, Craig's critique of Talbott's standard is weak, appealing only to morally acceptable cases of human deceptions, which hardly suffice to demonstrate that God would be similarly justified in such extreme eternal deceptions as hiding truths about the damnation of the loved ones of the redeemed. I am inclined to call this debate a draw due to an impasse of conflicting intuitions.

Fortunately, however, this does not mean that the question of the reasonableness of the selective amnesia solution is undecidable. There is another reason to question this approach which has nothing to do with the question of the moral legitimacy of divine deception and everything to do with the impact of memory obliteration on the redeemed themselves. At least when it comes to loved ones who are close family members, such as a parent, child, or sibling, memory erasure would demand such a deep and radical restructuring of one's memories that it would constitute revising one's personal identity. Consider for a moment how many of your memories involve or are built around your parents and their influence on you. Thorough removal of memories of one of them would not only be significant in itself but would necessitate alteration or removal of countless other memories of people you know who had close relationships to them, including your other parent, your siblings, and numerous other extended family members. In short, such selective amnesia could not be accomplished in a surgical way when it regarded a close loved one but would involve a significant change in who you are as a person.

---

from eternal blessedness, see Reitan, "Eternal Damnation," 431–32.

8. Craig, "Talbott's Universalism," 306.
9. Talbott, "Craig on the Possibility," 509.

Hell and Divine Goodness

It might seem to be an overreaching critique to suggest that the selective amnesia solution creates a problem of personal identity. But anyone familiar with cases of severe amnesia will recognize the appropriateness of this claim. To take a case from many years ago, a teenage girl was found wandering the streets of Sacramento who had no idea who or where she was. After she was identified and reunited with her family, her parents were distraught to discover that their daughter didn't recognize them and had no recollection of her home, her boyfriend, or anything about her previous life. And since her memory loss was permanent, the girl's parents had to educate her from scratch about her entire life. In describing the situation, the mother declared that her daughter was "a completely different person." More recently, former NFL player Scott Bolzan lost all of his memories because of a head trauma. Consequently, he has had to relearn his entire life history and restart all of his closest relationships. Bolzan sums up his experience by saying "I lost who I am."[10] Given permanent, global memory loss, such language is hardly hyperbolic. Severe amnesia restructures personal identity,[11] and this is a devastating loss, both for the amnesiac and her loved ones.

Now compare the partial amnesiac who only fails to recall certain close friends and loved ones. To effect this change, huge swaths of memory would have to be purged. So the effect would be severe and differ only in degree from the two persons described above. For the person who was the only one in her family who was ultimately redeemed, the amnesia effect would be especially dramatic. Although we couldn't say that such a person in heaven is "a completely different person," we would have to say that her personal identify has changed severely in a negative sense.[12] And this would be a terrible loss—the sort of extreme loss that seems utterly inconsistent with any plausible account of heavenly bliss. So it appears the

---

10. Bob Woodruff and Melia Patria, "Man with Amnesia." Bolzan, who eventually became CEO of the company Legendary Jets, authored a book recounting his experience. See *My Life Deleted*.

11. I am assuming here that, at least as far as conscious, rational beings are concerned, John Locke is roughly correct when he says that a necessary condition for personal identity through time is sameness of consciousness, and the maintenance of memories is essential for this. See his *An Essay concerning Human Understanding*, II, 27, 9–10.

12. Talbott briefly anticipates the critique I offer here when he asserts regarding this selective amnesia theory, "I doubt that Craig has any conception of how much of a person's mind that would destroy" ("Craig on the Possibility," 508). So too, in more detail, does MacDonald (Parry), *The Evangelical Universalist*, 16–17.

selective amnesia approach is really not a solution to the problem of heavenly grief.

The Beatific Vision Approach

When it comes to the problem of heavenly grief, the selective amnesia approach is not the only proposal made by William Lane Craig. In fact, his preferred solution seems to be an appeal to beatific vision where the saved will be so enraptured in God's love that they will feel no sorrow or sense of loss. Craig explains,

> It is possible that the very experience itself of being in the immediate presence of Christ (cf. the beatific vision) will simply drive from the minds of His redeemed any awareness of the lost in hell. So overwhelming will be His presence and the love and joy which it inspires that the knowledge of the damned will be banished from the consciousness of God's people. In such a case, the redeemed would still have such knowledge, but they would never be conscious of it and so never pained by it.[13]

There are two major problems with this theory. First, Craig appears to be inconsistent in his claims, since, on the one hand, he proposes regarding awareness of the lost that God will eliminate this from the minds of the redeemed, so that it will be "banished from [their] consciousness." On the other hand, Craig insists that the redeemed will nonetheless "still have such knowledge." But how can one have this knowledge and yet "never be conscious of it"? The juxtaposition of these two claims seems incoherent. Surely, to have knowledge of any factual matter, especially a fact so important as the eternal destiny of a loved one, is also to be consciously aware of it, at least sometimes during one's eternal existence. If one is never aware of this, then how can Craig call it genuine "knowledge"? But if it is not something that is truly known, as his proposal actually seems to entail, then this beatific vision theory really just collapses back into the selective amnesia approach.

A further problem with Craig's beatific vision theory regards how we should think about the moral effects of such an intimate personal experience of the beauty and goodness of God. It is natural to assume that this kind of immediate encounter with God would greatly increase a person's

---

13. Craig, "Talbott's Universalism," 307.

love and concern for others. But Craig's proposal seems to assume otherwise. As Talbott puts it, "It is possible that the beatific vision will drive all knowledge of the lost from the consciousness of the redeemed (without obliterating it altogether) only if is possible that the beatific vision will make the redeemed less loving and thus more calloused."[14] But, of course, it is absurd to suggest that the beatific vision could have such a negative effect on the redeemed. This whole approach seems to assume a very insular view of beatific vision, where the essential effect of religious rapture is to close one off from concern and awareness of fellow human beings, as opposed to heightening and enriching that awareness. Given that so much of Christian moral-spiritual development on earth—coinciding with our increasing communion with God—is about deepening and expanding awareness of others, it is counter-intuitive to suppose that our close approach to God in the eschaton would radically *diminish* that awareness of some people, even including many of those whom we deeply loved on earth. Otherwise put, if beatific vision is essentially a perfect human union with God,[15] and God is ever and always lovingly concerned with human beings, then the beatific vision should increase our loving awareness of others, not decrease it, and this includes our loving awareness of the lost.

The Love Reorientation Approach

A better way to deal with the problem of heavenly grief might be to appeal not so much to forgetfulness or decreased awareness of the lost as to a certain *reorientation of affections*. Thus, perhaps when we arrive in heaven we stop loving our friends and loved ones who have been damned. We retain all of our memories of them, including the fact that we loved them, even very intensely. But our love toward them itself disappears. Popular author Randy Alcorn takes this approach, which accounts for this loss of love by proposing that the damned will become *unlovable*: "What we loved in those who died without Christ was God's beauty we once saw in them. When God forever withdraws from them, I think they'll no longer bear his image and no longer reflect his beauty. Although they will be the same people, without God they'll be stripped of all the qualities we loved.

---

14. Talbott, "Craig on the Possibility," 510.

15. Here I am following the traditional Thomistic account of beatific vision as an immediate knowledge of God or a grasping of the divine essence. See *Summa Theologica*, I-II.q3.a8.

Therefore, paradoxically, in a sense they will not be the people we loved."[16] For Alcorn, the damned are transformed in a way that is antithetical to the transformation of the redeemed in heaven. Whereas the latter are perfected in virtue and become deserving objects of love, the damned lose all remnants of goodness and thus deserve nothing but contempt. Therefore, it is appropriate for the redeemed in heaven to hate them and desire their torment, even though on earth they deeply loved some of these persons.

Richard Swinburne appears to endorse a similar view of the matter when he says that the damned completely lose their capacity to make virtuous choices:

> We may describe a man in this situation of having lost his capacity to overrule his desires as having "lost his soul." Such a man is a prisoner of bad desires. He can no longer choose to resist them by doing the action which he judges to be overall the best thing to do. He has no natural desires to do the actions of heaven and he cannot choose to do them because he sees them to be of supreme worth. There is no "he" left to make that choice.[17]

There are problems with this approach. First, to assume, as Alcorn does, that someone could stop bearing the image of God yet remain the "same" person is dubious, if not unintelligible. But even granting this, it fails to solve the core problem, for it does not address one basic dimension of heavenly grief: *the loss of our loved ones*. Stripping a person of their beauty, goodness, and even *imago Dei* is horribly sad and tragic, as is the prospect of someone being imprisoned by their bad desires, even if this is deserved. The fact that there would be nothing left to love in one's close friend or family member would itself be cause for tremendous grief.

In fact, the fate of the damned in these scenarios seems more sad and tragic than that proposed on the previous accounts, for not only do the saints in heaven lose their relationship with their loved ones in hell but now they must also deal with the fact that their loved ones have been dehumanized, transformed into something monstrous and ugly. One thinks of a zombie film where a man's wife is caught and killed by the zombie hoard encroaching on his property. As if that's not bad enough, a few scenes later as he is fending off the zombies he discovers to his horror that his wife is now among them, mindlessly but relentlessly pursuing him to make a meal of his brain. Surely this disturbing transformation only makes the situation

16. Alcorn, "If Our Loved Ones Are in Hell."
17. Swinburne, "Theodicy," 49.

more dreadful. Likewise, the monstrous and tragic transformation of one's loved ones in hell. Yet Alcorn's proposal asks us to be comforted by it?

The Greater Joy by Contrast Approach

The standard Christian account of heaven sees it as a condition of immense joy largely due to the grace experienced by all who are there. Some theologians have claimed that such joy can only be fully appreciated in light of the damnation that the saints have *avoided*. And some have leveraged this point so as to suggest that the joy of heaven will actually be augmented as we behold the suffering of the damned. One vivid example is Jonathan Edwards, who writes:

> When the saints in glory . . . shall see the doleful state of the damned, how will this heighten their sense of blessedness of their own state, so exceedingly different from it! When they shall see how miserable others of their fellow-creatures are, who were naturally in the same circumstances with themselves; when they shall see the smoke of their torment, and the raging of the flames of their burning, and hear their dolorous shrieks and cries, and consider that they in the meantime are in the most blissful state, and shall surely be in it to all eternity; how will they rejoice![18]

Such thinking is deeply repellent even to many traditionalists. We may question Edwards' claim that seeing the calamities of others tends to heighten the sense of our own enjoyments. Granted, there is something to the idea that we better appreciate many of our blessings through contrast. However, this is only true in some cases and to a certain degree. Thus, for instance, I take greater pleasure in the endurance of my Toyota Corolla, which has accumulated over 400,000 miles on the original engine, when I observe others' cars tapping out at a mere 150,000 miles. And my sense

---

18. Edwards, "The End of the Wicked," 209. The same attitude has been expressed by contemporary scholars such as John Gerstner, who writes,

> Even *now*, while the evangelical is singing the praises of his Lord and savior, Jesus Christ, he knows that multitudes are suffering the torments of the damned. He knows that Judas Iscariot has been in unimaginable agony of soul for two thousand years, and that the worst of all torments will be that after his buried body is raised from his bones and ashes he will suffer in body and soul forever and ever. The true Christian, aware of this, is happily, exuberantly, gladly praising the Judge of the Last Day, Jesus Christ, who has sentenced to such merited damnation millions of souls.
>
> (*Repent or Perish*, 32)

of blessedness as a fan of the recent World Series champion Chicago Cubs is heightened when I contemplate the recurrent heartbreak and woe that plagued that franchise for more than a century. But do we take greater joy in our health when we see a friend emaciated and in agony in the latter stages of pancreatic cancer? In seeing a basketball player suffer a compound fracture, do I take greater joy in my own sturdy limbs? Not at all. I am too preoccupied with painful empathy even to experience joy. Likewise, and *a fortiori*, it is hard to imagine how observing the damned suffer could evoke anything but distress and sorrow.

Now suppose there is something to Edwards' point here—that the joy of heaven could be increased by a clearer sense of the contrasting fate of those in hell. It seems this could be as effectively achieved through finite suffering of the damned, followed by annihilation. There is nothing specifically about eternal conscious torment that could endow the saved with a greater sense of their blessing than could be provided by a long but finite period of torment. Seeing the "smoke" of the torments of the wicked and knowing what this entailed for them would be sufficient. And since the saints in heaven would know that the destruction of the damned is complete (because of their annihilation), there would be no distressful empathy to undermine their joy. So to the extent that this approach to the problem of heavenly grief has any usefulness, it holds much more promise for the conditionalist than for the traditionalist.

The Concession to Heavenly Sorrow Approach

If all of the proposed solutions to the problem of heavenly grief considered thus far are failures, then we might be tempted to concede the unavoidability of a certain amount of pain and sorrow for the redeemed in heaven, depending on how many of their loved ones are condemned to hell. Such is Jerry Walls' response to the problem. He proposes that

> It may well be the case that there is nothing incoherent in the idea that perfect human bliss includes a "disturbing element." Of course, the disturbing element could not be predominant and the term may, in fact, be too strong a description. But the blessed may share the moral attitude of regret toward their fellow persons who reject the joy of God's kingdom. In short, the blessed may share God's perspective and consequently share God's perfect happiness,

a happiness which could be compatible with some element of suffering.[19]

Walls is to be commended for presumably recognizing the insufficiency of the sorts of attempts to solve the problem of heavenly grief already discussed. But the sort of concession he advocates is also deeply problematic. For one thing, it assumes divine passibility, the view that God has genuine emotions and can even suffer, much like we humans do. This is a minority position in the history of Christian theology and has been rejected by many leading Christian theologians.[20]

Even granting divine passibility and the possibility that the redeemed in heaven mirror God in experiencing some negative emotions in that blessed state, Walls' treatment of the problem understates the severity of the negative emotions that would surely plague the redeemed in heaven who have loved ones in hell, especially those who have lost many close friends and family members. Recalling my earlier analogy about being on an ocean cruise while your mother suffers in solitary confinement, the awareness of this horrible fact could hardly be described as a mere "disturbing element" in an otherwise enjoyable vacation. On the contrary, the entire experience would be ruined because you would be so preoccupied with the thought of her torment. Similarly, it is difficult to imagine that your heavenly joy would not be fundamentally undermined by the knowledge that persons whom you dearly love are in hell.

Walls also understates the problem by placing heavenly grief for the lost into the category of a "moral attitude of regret" regarding those who are lost to hell. This fails to capture the depth of sorrow one would feel both for loved ones in torment as well as for the sense of personal loss at the permanent severing of significant relationships. Our emotions of deep grief are not mere "moral attitudes," nor are they adequately described as regret, though regret for a loved one's stubborn resistance to Christ would surely constitute a part of that grief. Rather, such grief would surely involve deep and abiding sorrow which would be unrelenting because of the hopeless finality of our loved one's permanent fate, made far worse from the

---

19. Walls, *Hell*, 110.

20. For a good recent critique of divine passibility, see Weinandy, *Does God Suffer?* I am somewhat sympathetic with the idea of divine passibility, though I affirm a view I call "divine omnipathos," which aims to preserve divine immutability while at the same time affirming genuine divine emotion. For a discussion of this idea and the broader question of divine emotion see *Benefits of Providence*, 151–82.

perspective of the traditionalist, as one would have to endure the awareness that the torment of their loved ones must continue unceasingly.

Finally, it should also be noted that Walls' account appears problematic from a biblical standpoint. Scripture tells us, "[God] will wipe every tear from their eyes. There will be no more death or mourning or crying or pain, for the old order of things has passed away" (Rev 21:4). But, surely, if anything would be cause for mourning, pain, and tears it would be the knowledge that someone I dearly love is being tormented in hell without any chance of escape. How, then, can the biblical promise of a sorrow-free eschaton be squared with Walls' concession that there will be an "element of suffering" in heaven experienced by friends and loved ones of the damned? Something must give here, and I am inclined to trust the biblical promise rather than Walls' theory.

The Love-Web Approach

All of the approaches to solving the problem of heavenly grief considered thus far have something in common. In addition to being entirely speculative, each attempts to preclude heavenly grief by somehow adjusting the *perspective of the redeemed*, such as by reorienting their view of lost loved ones, changing their assessment of God's justice, or eliminating many of their memories. None of these approaches appear very promising as ultimate solutions to the problem. However, there is an alternative approach, which, though also speculative, avoids the besetting difficulties with these theories. This alternative solution challenges a crucial premise of the problem of heavenly grief, namely that among the residents of hell will be loved ones of the redeemed. What if this assumption turns out to be false? It is possible that all of those people who were loved by the redeemed eventually find their way to salvation and eternal life in heaven, even if for some the route to redemption runs through hell. This is not to suggest that universalism is true. Rather, this is only to suggest that none of those who are ultimately damned were ever loved ones of the redeemed. On this view, all of the redeemed constitute a closed community or "web" of love, such that everyone who loves or is loved by a redeemed person will ultimately find salvation.

A natural response to this suggestion is that, from a statistical standpoint, it is highly unlikely. But God is a miracle worker, able to achieve outcomes that surprise and defy all odds. There is a variety of ways in which

Hell and Divine Goodness

God could accomplishes this, such as by ensuring the salvation in this life of all of those in the web or by ensuring that anyone sent to hell who was loved by a redeemed person is finally restored to God. This latter permutation of the love-web view would affirm a limited, non-universalist brand of restorationism. And, like the universalist version of the view, it would ensure that no one in heaven would grieve the permanent loss of a loved one and would thereby solve the problem of heavenly grief without selling the eschatological farm to the universalist.

While not directly taught in Scripture, biblical support for the idea may be found in Jesus' comment to Peter in Matthew 16:19: "I will give you the keys of the kingdom of heaven; whatever you bind on earth will be bound in heaven, and whatever you loose on earth will be loosed in heaven." Could it be that the keys to which Jesus refers here consist essentially in love? Another passage pointing in this direction is a statement Jesus makes during one of his resurrection appearances. He says to his disciples, "If you forgive anyone's sins, their sins are forgiven; if you do not forgive them, they are not forgiven" (John 20:23). While the scope of the sins forgivable by his disciples is not specified here, the fact that he gives them the authority to forgive others' sins at all provides some support for the love-web concept. After all, love is epitomized in forgiveness and other acts of grace.

While the love-web approach constitutes an advance over the previously considered views, it is not without its difficulties. First, it assumes that there are clear demarcations between those we love and those we do not love, whereas in real life our affections for other people seem to work on a continuum, from lesser to greater degrees of love. So the web of love, it would seem, is not so easily determined. To this concern, however, the love-web proponent may simply grant that even the slightest trace of Christian love would be sufficient to ensure the salvation of the spiritually beloved. This would be enough to guarantee non-arbitrary clear lines between the saved and the damned.[21]

But here arises another potential objection to the view, namely that it puts too much power of salvation into the hands of human beings. Aren't the redeemed *God's* elect, rather than the elect of those Christians who happened to extend love to them? Well, one might reply, that's just part of what is meant by Jesus' words in Matthew 16—God has made Christians

---

21. Jesus' remarks in John 20:23 are noteworthy here in that his statement is straightforwardly binary, rather than nuanced in terms of degrees. One either forgives another's sins or one does not, and, accordingly, they are forgiven or they are not.

deputies of divine election. But the problem with this, one might further object, is that it makes salvation too capricious—making certain people's salvation reliant on the will and affections of other humans. For the Calvinist, this problem can be explained away in terms of a high view of providence by insisting that God sovereignly governs whom we love anyway, so the ultimate recipients of salvation are no less God's elect even though he uses the secondary cause of human love to secure the salvation of some. The Arminian, on the other hand, may simply concede the point that there is a certain amount of blessed serendipity that God builds into his system of salvation, as some fortunate souls become unwitting benefactors of Christian love. For those Arminians who are uncomfortable with this, however, the love-web approach will likely be less attractive.

Another objection to this approach may be based on the idea that heavenly bliss necessarily entails love for all people, an assumption routinely made by universalists. Thus, Schleiermacher says that in heaven our "sympathy must be such as to embrace the whole human race."[22] Thomas Talbott asserts that the redeemed person is "filled with love for others and therefore desires the good for all other created persons."[23] And Eric Reitan declares, "anyone in a state of eternal blessedness possesses both perfect bliss and universal love for all persons."[24] But why assume that the love of the redeemed in heaven must be universal? It is possible, after all, that God does not love every human being, and those whom he never loved will not be saved. Such is the classical Calvinist take on the matter, and for all we know, that might be correct, in which case the love displayed by the redeemed in heaven might match that of God in being so limited and thus sidestep the objection. But even if God does love all human beings, it doesn't follow that in heaven we must have the same depth of love that God has for every human being. As discussed in the previous chapter, as finite beings our loves must always be limited and somewhat selective. So our love for family members and good friends on earth would presumably be far more personal and intense than the sort of general "sympathy" for humankind to which Schleiermacher refers, assuming he is correct in this. Such non-personal sympathy is much less of a threat to heavenly bliss, if it is a threat at all. But, again, we need not assume this much.

---

22. Schleiermacher, *Christian Faith*, 721.
23. Talbott, "Providence, Freedom, and Human Destiny," 239.
24. Reitan, "Sympathy for the Damned," 202.

Why must we accept Schleiermacher's assumption that the perfection of our nature in heaven necessarily generates a universal sympathy for humankind? Schleiermacher suggests that the "perfecting of our nature" in heaven would entail a universal love, because the blessed state would constitute a genuine advance from our earthly state. Eric Reitan expands on this idea, noting that, "someone who is universally loving (as we assume the blessed to be) would identify with *all* persons. For such a person, to be *supremely* happy is to approve of the state or condition of all persons—an approval that, given Christian assumptions, would arise only if the person believed that every person were united with God in love."[25] Both Reitan and Schleiermacher make problematic assumptions here. First, Reitan assumes that the redeemed in heaven will be universally loving. Again, why assume this? If God himself does not eternally love all people, then the extension of the love of the redeemed would be similarly restricted to match the extension of divine love. As for Schleiermacher, he assumes that our advance from the earthly state to the heavenly state necessarily entails universal sympathy with other people. But this is a non-sequitur. Surely our sympathies will advance considerably in that state, but even the extension of our deep affections from hundreds or thousands to, say, billions of fellow redeemed souls will constitute an enormous advance in our capacity to love. Schleiermacher is simply mistaken in assuming that anything less than universal love for humanity would be a "move backwards" for the redeemed.

So we need not grant the premise of those who would challenge the love-web approach by appealing to the notion that the redeemed in heaven must love everyone. The love-web solution, then, remains a live option for non-universalists in dealing with the problem of heavenly grief. While not without its challenges, it appears to be less problematic than the other ways of dealing with the problem discussed above.

CONCLUSION

Two overarching lessons may be drawn from the discussion in this chapter. First, the problem of heavenly grief is a significant challenge for non-universalist accounts of hell, especially the traditional view. Yet, secondly, the problem does not amount to a decisive argument in favor of universalism. All of the proposed solutions we have considered have their difficulties, but

25. Ibid., 206.

it seems to me that the love-web approach is the most promising among them, as it avoids numerous disturbing implications of other approaches (e.g., regarding negatively altered personal identities of the redeemed, problematic moral implications regarding enjoyment of the agony of the damned, and concessions that the redeemed in heaven may experience pain and suffering). The love-web approach has the further merit of affirming the intuition that our love for others remains constant beyond the grave. It also affirms that our love for others has salvific power, no matter who is the recipient. This is a bold claim, to be sure, but perhaps it is simply to take seriously the biblical promise that "love never fails" (1 Cor 13:8).

Conclusion

Now that we have concluded our study of the doctrine of hell, some summary remarks are in order. Our look at the biblical evidence in the first chapter revealed that each of the three views of hell enjoys at least some biblical support. Given that the early church fathers were so divided on the issue of hell, this is just what we should expect to be the case. As for the evidence for each view, we found that the biblical arguments are generally weak, though two passages in Revelation (20:10 and 14:10–11) do pose a challenge for the non-traditionalist views. We saw that there are several good biblical arguments for conditionalism, especially those which appeal to (1) the biblical imagery of fire (Isa 33:12; Mal 4:1–3, etc.), (2) the numerous references to the destruction of the wicked (Isa 66; 2 Pet 2:6, etc.) and (3) the pervasive biblical theme of opposition between life and death (Prov 12:28; John 3:16, etc.). As for universalism, we found that arguments from such biblical themes as (1) God's reconciling all things to himself (Col 1:20), (2) the parallels between the two Adams (1 Cor 15:22 and Rom 5:12–19), and (3) God's desire for all to be saved (e.g. Rom 11:32, 1 Tim 2:4, etc.) provide *prima facie* evidence for the view. But we also saw that there are good non-traditionalist responses to these passages. Furthermore, the biblical teachings regarding election (Rom 11:7; 2 Tim 2:10, etc.) and the unforgivable sin (Matt 12:31–32) create significant problems for universalism.

Thus, on the whole, the biblical witness seems to favor the conditionalist view. But the evidence is hardly decisive, which underscores the need for careful philosophical reflection on this issue, such as I attempted to provide in the remainder of the book. In chapter 2 we analyzed the three views of hell in light of considerations of justice, specifically the proportionality criterion, according to which the severity of a punishment must match the severity of the offense. We found that the traditional doctrine of hell as eternal conscious torment fails this criterion miserably as all of

Conclusion

the routes available to the traditionalist to justify the doctrine of ECT are failures. Also in this chapter we found that there are good reasons to think that annihilation of the soul is a more severe punishment than ECT, which undermines the common traditionalist claim that ECT is the most severe punishment possible.

Chapter 3 compared the various perspectives on hell in terms of their respective capacities for dealing with the problem of evil as it relates to the doctrine of hell. We found that the traditional view suffers from a far more serious problem of evil than the non-traditional views, as it entails that in hell there is (1) eternal natural evil in the form of unending suffering of the damned and (2) eternal moral evil in the form of either (a) infinite human guilt (IGT) or (b) perpetually continuous human sin (CST). And as for eternal moral evil, whether one affirms IGT or CST, the traditional view implies that moral evil (an infinite amount, given IGT) remains unpunished forever, an implication that contradicts the biblical teaching that God will fully conquer evil and reconcile all things to himself. Finally, in this chapter we also explored the prospects of the free-will defense (FWD) and the soul-making theodicy (SMT) for assisting proponents of the three views in dealing with the problem of hell. We found that these approaches are of no help to the traditionalist, most helpful to the universalist, and mildly helpful to the conditionalist. But we also noted that given the potential justice of terminal punishment—finite suffering in hell followed by annihilation—the conditionalist might not even need to appeal to the FWD, SMT, or any other means of accounting for evil in order to adequately deal with the problem of evil concerning hell.

Chapter 4 explored issues related to human immortality and salvation. We discussed three different arguments that aim to demonstrate the natural immortality of human beings and found that all of these fail. Next, we looked at several philosophical arguments against universalism and concluded that three of these arguments—specifically, those that appeal to the meaning of salvation, human freedom, and divine freedom—reveal serious problems for universalism. This chapter concluded with a brief consideration of the concept of post-mortem opportunities for salvation, and we found that there appear to be no good reasons to reject this possibility and some grounds for supporting it, regardless of which of the three perspectives on hell one affirms.

In the fifth chapter, we discussed the problem of heavenly grief, which universalists sometimes deploy as a critique of non-universalist views of hell. We discussed six common approaches to dealing with the problem, specifically appeals to pleasing justice, selective amnesia, beatific vision, love reorientation, greater joy by contrast, and the concession to heavenly sorrow. We found that each of these approaches to the problem of heavenly grief has significant problems. Therefore, I proposed an original alternative way of dealing with the problem—the "love-web" theory, which overcomes the difficulties with the other approaches and also seems to enjoy some independent biblical support from such passages as Matthew 16:19 and John 20:23.

This book is far from an exhaustive discussion of the subject of hell. But relative to the issues discussed here, the conditionalist perspective is the most plausible view among the three major alternatives. Biblically speaking, conditionalism enjoys more evidential warrant than traditionalism and universalism. And philosophically, conditionalism is far more defensible than traditionalism and somewhat more defensible than universalism. Another way of putting this is to say that, on the whole—considering both the biblical and philosophical evidence—conditionalism has the most explanatory power among the three views of hell—again, at least in light of the issues discussed here.

Throughout this study I have strived to remain as fair and even-handed as possible, despite my convictions in favor of the conditionalist view. Along the way, this resolve has enabled me to better appreciate the arguments for traditionalism and, especially, universalism, which is the view that I most strongly *hope* to be true. While I remain a convinced conditionalist, my mind is open, and I expect that however my views might develop on this issue, I will never be dogmatic or terribly confident in my epistemic stance. That is, my convictions on this issue are (I think) humble and gently held. But I am *very* confident of this: the day is coming when the truth about this and so many other theological issues will be made clear to all of us—when Christ returns in glory and inaugurates his reign on a new heaven and a new earth. Amen.

Bibliography

Adams, Marilyn M. "Aesthetic Goodness as a Solution to the Problem of Evil." In *God, Truth, and Reality: Essays in Honor of John Hick*, edited by Arvind Sharma, 46–61. New York: St. Martin's, 1993.

———. "Hell and the God of Justice." *Religious Studies* 11 (1975) 433–47.

———. "The Problem of Hell: A Problem of Evil for Christians." In *Reasoned Faith: Essays in Philosophical Theology in Honor of Norman Kretzmann*, edited by Eleonore Stump, 301–27. Ithaca, NY: Cornell University Press, 1993.

Adams, Robert M. "Middle Knowledge and the Problem of Evil." *American Philosophical Quarterly* 14 (1977) 109–17.

Akin, Daniel L. *1, 2, 3 John*. Nashville: Broadman & Holman, 2001.

Alcorn, Randy. "If Our Loved Ones Are in Hell, Won't That Spoil Heaven?" *Eternal Perspective Ministries* (March 26, 2010). http://www.epm.org/resources/2010/Mar/26/if-our-loved-ones-are-hell-wont-spoil-heaven/.

Aquinas, Thomas. *Summa Theologica*. Volumes 1–3. Translated by the English Dominican Fathers. New York: Benziger Brothers, 1947.

Argyle, A. W. *The Gospel according to Matthew*. Cambridge: Cambridge University Press, 1963.

Aristotle. *Nicomachean Ethics*. Translated by W. D. Ross. In *The Basic Works of Aristotle*. Edited by Richard McKeon. New York: Random House, 1941.

Arminius, James. "Disputation 17." In *The Writings of James Arminius*. Vol. 2. Translated by James Nichols 36–39. Grand Rapids: Baker, 1956.

Atkinson, Basil F. C. "The Doom of the Lost." In *Rethinking Hell: Readings in Evangelical Conditionalism*, edited by C. M. Date, G. G. Stump, and J. W. Anderson, 99–115. Eugene OR: Cascade, 2014.

Augustine. *The City of God*. Translated by Marcus Dods. New York: Random House, 1993.

———. *Confessions and Enchiridion*. Edited and translated by A. C. Outler. Philadelphia: Westminster, 1955.

Barclay, William. *The Letters to the Philippians, Colossians, and Thessalonians*. Rev. ed. Philadelphia: Westminster, 1975.

Bawulski, Shawn. "Annihilationism, Traditionalism, and the Problem of Hell." *Philosophia Christi* 12 (2010) 61–79.

Beale, G. K. *The Book of Revelation: A Commentary on the Greek Text*. Grand Rapids: Eerdmans, 1999.

Bolzan, Scott. *My Life Deleted: A Memoir*. New York: HarperCollins, 2011.

Bibliography

Boring, M. E. "The Language of Universal Salvation in Paul." *Journal of Biblical Literature* 105 (1986) 269–92.

Bowles, Ralph G. "Does Revelation 14:11 Teach Eternal Torment?" In *Rethinking Hell: Readings in Evangelical Conditionalism*, edited by C. M. Date, G. G. Stump, and J. W. Anderson, 138–54. Eugene OR: Cascade, 2014.

Brown, Claire, and Jerry L. Walls. "Annihilationism: A Philosophical Dead End?" In *The Problem of Hell: A Philosophical Anthology*, edited by Joel Buenting, 45–64. Aldershot, UK: Ashgate, 2010.

Buckareff, Andrei A., and Allen Plug. "Escaping Hell: Divine Motivation and the Problem of Hell." *Religious Studies* 41 (2005) 39–54.

Burk, Denny. "Eternal Conscious Torment." In *Four Views on Hell*, edited by Preston Sprinkle, 17–43. Grand Rapids: Zondervan, 2016.

Cain, James. "Is the Existence of Heaven Compatible with the Existence of Hell?" *Southwest Philosophy Review* 18 (2002) 153–58.

———. "On the Problem of Hell." *Religious Studies* 38 (2002) 355–62.

Calvin, John. *Commentary on the Prophet Isaiah*. Vol. 3. Grand Rapids: Baker, 2005.

———. *Institutes of the Christian Religion*. Translated by Ford L. Battles. Philadelphia: Westminster, 1960.

Carson, D. A. *The Gagging of God: Christianity Confronts Pluralism*. Grand Rapids: Zondervan, 1996.

Constable, Henry. "Divine Justice." In *Rethinking Hell: Readings in Evangelical Conditionalism*, edited by C. M. Date, G. G. Stump, and J. W. Anderson, 198–206. Eugene OR: Cascade, 2014.

Copleston, Frederick. *A History of Philosophy*. Vol. 2. New York: Doubleday, 1993.

Cowan, Steven B. "The Grounding Objection to Middle Knowledge Revisited." *Religious Studies* 39 (2003) 93–102.

Craig, William L. "'No Other Name': A Middle Knowledge Perspective on the Exclusivity of Salvation through Christ." *Faith and Philosophy* 6 (1989) 172–88.

———. "Talbott's Universalism." *Religious Studies* 27 (1991) 297–308.

Cranfield, C. E. B. *Romans: A Shorter Commentary*. Grand Rapids: Eerdmans, 1985.

Creel, Richard E. *Divine Impassibility*. Cambridge: Cambridge University Press, 1986.

Crisp, Oliver D. "Divine Retribution: A Defence." *Sophia* 42 (2003) 35–52.

Dabney, Robert L. *Lectures in Systematic Theology*. Grand Rapids: Zondervan, 1972.

Davidson, Donald. "How Is Weakness of the Will Possible?" In *Moral Concepts*, edited by Joel Feinberg, 93–113. Oxford: Oxford University Press, 1970.

de Boer, Martinus C. *The Defeat of Death: Apocalyptic Eschatology in 1 Corinthians 15 and Romans 15*. Sheffield, UK: Sheffield Academic Press, 1988.

DeRose, Keith. "Universalism and the Bible: The Really Good News." http://campuspress.yale.edu/keithderose/1129-2/#7.

DeWeese, Garry. "Natural Evil: A 'Free Process' Defense." In *God and Evil: The Case for God in a World Filled with Pain*, edited by Chad Meister and James K. Dew Jr., 53–64. Downers Grove, IL: InterVarsity, 2013.

Edwards, Jonathan. "The End of the Wicked Contemplated by the Righteous." In *The Works of Jonathan Edwards*, Vol. 2, edited by John E. Smith, 207–12. Edinburgh: Banner of Truth Trust, 1974.

———. "The Justice of God in the Damnation of Sinners." In *The Works of Jonathan Edwards*. Vol. 19, edited by M. X. Lesser, 336–76. New Haven, CT: Yale University Press, 2001.

Bibliography

Erickson, Millard J. *Christian Theology*. Vol. 3. Grand Rapids: Baker, 1985.
Frame, John M. *No Other God: A Response to Open Theism*. Nashville: P&R, 2001.
Froom, Le Roy Edwin. *The Conditionalist Faith of Our Fathers*. Washington, DC: Review and Herald, 1966.
Fudge, Edward W. "The Case for Conditionalism." In *Two Views of Hell: A Biblical and Theological Dialogue*, 19–82. Downers Grove, IL: InterVarsity, 2000.
———. *The Fire that Consumes: A Biblical and Historical Study of the Doctrine of Final Punishment*. Rev. ed. Lincoln, NE: Authors Guild, 2001. (*The Fire That Consumes: A Biblical and Historical Study of the Doctrine of Final Punishment*. Fully updated, revised, and expanded 3rd ed. Eugene, OR: Cascade, 2011.)
Geach, Peter. *Providence and Evil*. Cambridge: Cambridge University Press, 1977.
Gerstner, John H. *Repent or Perish*. Ligonier, PA: Soli Deo Gloria, 1990.
Grudem, Wayne. *Systematic Theology: An Introduction to Biblical Doctrine*. Grand Rapids: Zondervan, 1994.
Guillebaud, Harold E. "The General Trend of Bible Teaching." In *Rethinking Hell: Readings in Evangelical Conditionalism*, edited by C. M. Date, G. G. Stump, and J. W. Anderson, 155–73. Eugene, OR: Cascade, 2014.
Hasker, William. *God, Time, and Knowledge*. Ithaca, NY: Cornell University Press, 1989.
Hay, David M. *Colossians*. Nashville: Abingdon, 2000.
Helm, Paul. "The Logic of Limited Atonement." *Scottish Bulletin of Evangelical Theology* 3 (1985) 47–54.
Hick, John. *Evil and the God of Love*. New York: Harper and Row, 1978.
Hillert, Sven. *Limited and Universal Salvation: A Text Oriented and Hermeneutical Study of Two Perspectives in Paul*. Stockholm: Almqvist & Wiksell, 1999.
Himma, Kenneth E. "Eternally Incorrigible: The Continuing-Sin Response to the Proportionality Problem of Hell." *Religious Studies* 39 (2003) 61–78.
Hodge, Charles. *Commentary on the Epistle to the Romans*. New York: Armstrong and Son, 1896.
Hughes, Philip E. "Is the Soul Immortal?" In *Rethinking Hell: Readings in Evangelical Conditionalism*, edited by C. M. Date, G. G. Stump, and J. W. Anderson, 185–97. Eugene, OR: Cascade, 2014.
Hunt, David P. "Divine Providence and Simple Foreknowledge." *Faith and Philosophy* 10 (1993) 394–414.
Irenaeus. *Against Heresies*. In *Ante-Nicene Fathers*, edited by Alexander Roberts and James Donaldson, 315–567. Peabody, MA: Hendrickson, 1994.
Jewett, Robert. *Romans: A Commentary*. Minneapolis: Fortress, 2007.
Jordan, Jeff. "The Topography of Divine Love." *Faith and Philosophy* 29 (2012) 53–69.
Kabay, Paul. "Is the Status Principle Beyond Salvation? Toward Redeeming an Unpopular Theory of Hell." *Sophia* 44 (2005) 91–103.
Käsemann, Ernst. *Commentary on Romans*. Translated by Geoffrey W. Bromiley. Grand Rapids: Eerdmans, 1980.
Keener, Craig. *Romans*. Eugene, OR: Cascade, 2009.
Kershnar, Stephen. "Hell and Punishment." In *The Problem of Hell: A Philosophical Anthology*, edited by Joel Buenting, 115–32. Aldershot, UK: Ashgate, 2010.
———. "The Injustice of Hell." *International Journal for Philosophy of Religion* 58 (2005) 103–23.
Kronen, John, and Eric Reitan. *God's Final Victory: A Comparative Philosophical Case for Universalism*. London: Continuum, 2011.

Bibliography

Küng, Hans. *Eternal Life?: Life After Death as a Medical, Philosophical, and Theological Problem*. Translated by Edward Quinn. Garden City, NY: Doubleday, 1984.
Kvanvig, Jonathan L. *The Problem of Hell*. New York: Oxford University Press, 1993.
Le Guin, Ursula. "The Ones Who Walk Away from Omelas." In *The Wind's Twelve Quarters and the Compass Rose*, 254–62. London: Orion, 1975.
Leibniz, Gottfried. *Philosophical Writings*. Translated by Mary Morris and G. H. Parkinson. London: Dent and Sons, 1973.
Lewis, C. S. *The Great Divorce*. New York: Macmillan, 1946.
———. *The Problem of Pain*. New York: Macmillan, 1962.
Lewis, David. "Divine Evil." In *Arguing About Religion*, edited by Kevin Timpe, 472–81. London: Routledge, 2009.
Locke, John. *An Essay Concerning Human Understanding*. Edited by Peter H. Nidditch. Oxford: Oxford University Press, 1975.
Lotz, David W. "Heaven and Hell in the Christian Tradition." *Religion in Life* 48 (1979) 77–90.
Lukes, Steven. "Moral Weakness." *The Philosophical Quarterly* 15 (1965) 104–14.
MacDonald, George. "Justice." In *The Heart of George MacDonald*, edited by Rolland Hein, 345–60. Wheaton, IL: Harold Shaw, 1994.
MacDonald, Gregory. *The Evangelical Universalist*. 1st ed. Eugene, OR: Cascade, 2006.
Mackie, J. L. "Evil and Omnipotence." *Mind* 64 (1955) 200–212.
Marshall, Christopher D. "Divine and Human Punishment in the New Testament." In *Rethinking Hell: Readings in Evangelical Conditionalism*, edited by C. M. Date, G. G. Stump, and J. W. Anderson, 207–27. Eugene OR: Cascade, 2014.
Marshall, I. Howard. *1 and 2 Thessalonians*. Grand Rapids: Eerdmans, 1983.
———. "Does the New Testament Teach Universal Salvation?" In *Called to One Hope: Perspectives on the Life to Come*, edited by J. Colwell, 17–30. Carlisle, UK: Paternoster, 2000.
McKnight, Scot. *The Letter to the Colossians*. Grand Rapids: Eerdmans, 2018.
McLeod-Harrison, Mark S. *The Resurrection of Immortality: An Essay in Philosophical Eschatology*. Eugene, OR: Cascade, 2017.
Miller, Stephen R. *Daniel*. Nashville: Broadman & Holman, 1994.
Molina, Luis de. *On Divine Foreknowledge: Part IV of the Concordia*. Translated by Alfred J. Freddoso. Ithaca, NY: Cornell University Press, 1988.
Moo, Douglas. *The Letter to the Colossians and to Philemon*. Grand Rapids: Eerdmans, 2008.
Morris, Leon. *The Epistle to the Romans*. Grand Rapids: Eerdmans, 1988.
Mortimore, Geoffrey, ed. *Weakness of Will*. London: MacMillan, 1971.
Murray, Michael J. "Heaven and Hell." In *Reason for the Hope Within*, edited by Michael J. Murray, 287–317. Grand Rapids: Eerdmans, 1999.
———. "Three Versions of Universalism." *Faith and Philosophy* 16 (1999) 55–68.
O'Brien, Peter T. *Word Bible Commentary, Vol. 44: Colossians and Philemon*. Waco, TX: Word, 1982.
Oden, Thomas C. *Life in the Spirit: Systematic Theology*. Vol. 3. Peabody MA: Prince, 1998.
Packer, J. I. "The Problem of Universalism Today." In *Celebrating the Saving Work of God*, 169–78. Carlisle, UK: Paternoster, 1998.
Peterson, Robert A. "The Case for Traditionalism." In *Two Views of Hell: A Biblical and Theological Dialogue*, 117–81. Downers Grove, IL: InterVarsity, 2000.

Bibliography

Pinnock, Clark. "The Destruction of the Finally Impenitent." In *Rethinking Hell: Readings in Evangelical Conditionalism*, edited by C. M. Date, G. G. Stump, and J. W. Anderson, 56–73. Eugene, OR: Cascade, 2014.

Plantinga, Alvin. *God, Freedom, and Evil*. Grand Rapids: Eerdmans, 1974.

———. *The Nature of Necessity*. Oxford: Clarendon, 1974.

Plato, *Phaedo*. Translated by Hugh Tredennick. In *The Collected Dialogues of Plato*, edited by Edith Hamilton and Huntington Cairns, 40–98. Princeton: Princeton University Press, 1961.

Reichenbach, Bruce R. *Evil and a Good God*. New York: Fordham University Press, 1982.

Reitan, Eric. "Eternal Damnation and Blessed Ignorance: Is the Damnation of Some Incompatible with the Salvation of Any?" *Religious Studies* 38 (2002) 429–50.

———. "Human Freedom and the Impossibility of Eternal Damnation." In *Universal Salvation? The Current Debate*, edited by Robin A. Parry and Christopher Partridge, 125–42. Grand Rapids: Eerdmans, 2003.

———. "Sympathy for the Damned: Schleiermacher's Critique of the Doctrine of Limited Salvation." *Southwest Philosophy Review* 18 (2002) 201–11.

Richards, Jay W. "A Pascalian Argument against Universalism." In *Unapologetic Apologetics*, edited by William A. Dembski and Jay W. Richards, 207–20. Downers Grove, IL: InterVarsity, 2001.

Sanders, John. *The God Who Risks: A Theology of Providence*. Downers Grove, IL: InterVarsity, 1998.

Saville, Andy. "Arguing with Annihilationism: An Assessment of the Doctrinal Arguments for Annihilationism." *Scottish Bulletin of Evangelical Theology* 24 (2006) 65–90.

Schleiermacher, Friedrich. *The Christian Faith*. 3rd ed. London: T. & T. Clark, 2016.

Schreiner, Thomas R. *Romans*. Grand Rapids: Baker, 1998.

Seymour, Charles. "Hell, Justice, and Freedom." *International Journal for Philosophy of Religion* 43 (1998) 69–86.

Shedd, W. G. T. *Dogmatic Theology*. 3rd ed. Phillipsburg, NJ: P&R Press, 2003.

Spiegel, James S. "Annihilation, Everlasting Torment, and Divine Justice." *International Journal of Philosophy and Theology* 76 (2015) 241–48.

———. *The Benefits of Providence: A New Look at Divine Sovereignty*. Wheaton, IL: Crossway, 2005.

———. "The Irenaean Soul-Making Theodicy." In *God and Evil: The Case for God in a World Filled with Pain*, edited by Chad Meister and James K. Dew Jr., 80–93. Downers Grove, IL: InterVarsity, 2013.

———. "On Free Will and Soul Making: Complementary Approaches to the Problem of Evil." *Philosophia Christi* 13 (2011) 405–13.

Stackhouse Jr., John G. "Terminal Punishment." In *Four Views on Hell*, edited by Preston Sprinkle, 61–81. Grand Rapids: Zondervan, 2016.

———. "A Terminal Punishment Response." In *Four Views on Hell*, edited by Preston Sprinkle, 44–47. Grand Rapids: Zondervan, 2016.

Stott, John. "Judgment and Hell." In *Rethinking Hell: Readings in Evangelical Conditionalism*, edited by C. M. Date, G. G. Stump, and J. W. Anderson, 48–55. Eugene, OR: Cascade, 2014.

———. *The Letters of John: An Introduction and* Commentary. Leicester, UK: InterVarsity, 1988.

———. *Romans: God's Good News for the World*. Downers Grove, IL: InterVarsity, 1994.

Bibliography

Stump, Eleonore. "Dante's Hell, Aquinas's Moral Theory and the Love of God." *Canadian Journal of Philosophy* 16 (1986) 181–98.

Swinburne, Richard. "Natural Evil." *American Philosophical Quarterly* 15 (1978) 295–301.

———. "A Theodicy of Heaven and Hell" in *The Existence and Nature of God*, edited by A. J. Freddoso, 37–54. Notre Dame, IN: University of Notre Dame Press, 1983.

Talbott, Thomas. "Craig on the Possibility of Eternal Damnation." *Religious Studies* 28 (1992) 495–510.

———. "The Doctrine of Everlasting Punishment." *Faith and Philosophy* 7 (1990) 19–42.

———. *The Inescapable Love of God*. 1st ed. Boca Raton, LA: Universal, 1999.

———. "Providence, Freedom, and Human Destiny." *Religious Studies* 26 (1990) 227–45.

———. "Punishment, Forgiveness, and Divine Justice." *Religious Studies* 29 (1993) 151–68.

———. "The Topography of Divine Love: A Response to Jeff Jordan." *Faith and Philosophy* 30 (2013) 302–16.

VanArragon, Raymond J. "Is It Possible to Freely Reject God Forever?" In *The Problem of Hell: A Philosophical Anthology*, edited by Joel Buenting, 29–43. Aldershot, UK: Ashgate, 2010.

Walls, Jerry L. *Hell: The Logic of Damnation*. Notre Dame, IN: University of Notre Dame Press, 1992.

Ware, Bruce. *God's Lesser Glory: The Diminished God of Open Theism*. Wheaton, IL: Crossway, 2000.

Weinandy, Thomas. *Does God Suffer?* Notre Dame, IN: University of Notre Dame Press, 2000.

Wenham, John W. "The Case for Conditional Immortality." In *Rethinking Hell: Readings in Evangelical Conditionalism*, edited by C. M. Date, G. G. Stump, and J. W. Anderson, 74–94. Eugene, OR: Cascade, 2014.

Wesley, John. *The Works of John Wesley*. Vol. 2. Nashville: Abingdon, 1985.

Witherington, Ben. *Paul's Letter to the Romans: A Socio-Rhetorical Commentary*. Grand Rapids: Eerdmans, 2004.

Woodruff, Bob, and Melia Patria, "Man with Amnesia Lost 46 Years in Workplace Slip." *ABC News* (April 19, 2010). https://abcnews.go.com/Nightline/amnesia-man-hits-head-loses-memories/story?id=10396719.

Index

Adams, Marilyn, 33n, 40–41, 58n, 64n, 99n, 127
Adams, Robert, 73n, 127
aiōnios, 11–12, 14–17
Akin, Daniel, 29n, 127
Alcorn, Randy, 114–16, 127
annihilation, xi, 2, 4n, 5–7, 13, 15, 18–20, 31–32, 34–35, 40, 47–54, 56, 60–61, 75, 77, 79, 81n, 85–86, 100, 103, 117, 125, 127–28, 131
Anselm of Canterbury, 3, 33n,
Aquinas, Thomas, 3–4, 34n, 39–41, 49n, 53, 82, 95, 104, 127, 132
Argyle, A. W, 12, 127
Aristotle, 93, 127
Arminian, 26n, 88, 121
Arminius, Jacob, 69, 127
Athenagoras of Athens, 3
Atkinson, Basil, 18, 127
atonement, 2, 7, 29–30, 54–55, 63, 87, 95n, 129
Augustine, 3, 8, 11, 36, 38n, 49, 57, 64n, 127
Augustinian, 49, 74–75

Barclay, William, 24n, 127
Barnabas of Alexandria, 3
Bawulski, Shawn, 4n, 40n, 47n, 48n, 50–51, 127
Beale, G. K., 15, 127
Bolzan, Scott, 112, 127
Boring, M. E., 27n, 128
Bowles, Ralph, 15n, 48n, 128
Brown, Claire, 4n, 128
Buckareff, Andrei, 101–3, 128

Burk, Denny, 9, 20, 128

Cain, James, 52, 107n, 128
Calvin, John, 3, 9, 38n,
Calvinism, 26n, 74–75, 87, 88, 100, 103, 121,
Carson, D. A., 45, 128,
Christ, Jesus, 7, 10, 12, 18, 20, 22, 24–25, 27–30, 37, 38n, 42n, 48n, 78, 81, 116n, 120
Clement of Rome, 3
compatiblism, 67, 74, 84, 94
Constable, Henry, 42n, 128
continuing-sin thesis, 43–46, 62–63, 73–75, 78, 125, 129
Copleston, Frederick, 82n, 128
Cowan, Steven, 73n, 128
Craig, William L., 71–73, 75, 110–11, 112n, 113–14, 128, 132
Cranfield, C. E. B., 27n, 128
Creel, Richard, 70, 128
Crisp, Oliver, 4n, 40n, 48n, 128

Dabney, Robert, 44n, 87n, 98–100, 104, 128
Dabney's Wager, 98–100
Davidson, Donald, 93n, 128
devil. *See* Satan.
de Boer, Martinus, 34n, 128
DeRose, Keith, 28n, 128
DeWeese, Garry, 64n, 128
Didymus of Alexandria, 3

Edwards, Jonathan, 3–4, 39–40, 116–17, 128

133

Index

elect, election (divine), 23, 26n, 29–31, 74, 87–88, 120–21, 124
Erickson, Millard, 28, 129
eternal conscious torment, 3, 5, 7–9, 14–15, 20, 32, 34–50, 53, 56, 59–62, 67–71, 74–75, 77–78, 80, 97, 99–100, 105, 117, 124–25, 128
Eusebius of Caesarea, 3
evangelism, 98–100, 103
evil, ix, xi, 1, 5–6, 17, 19, 21, 24, 26n, 35n, 39, 46, 49, 53, 55, 57–80, 83, 88–90, 92–93, 98–99, 105, 108, 125, 127–32

Frame, John, 70n, 129
free-will defense, 5, 64–68, 70, 72n, 73–76, 82–83, 90–91, 93, 125, 131
Froom, Le Roy, 3, 129
Fudge, Edward, xi, 12–13, 15–17, 129

Geach, Peter, 108–9, 129
Gerstner, John, 116, 129
Gomorrah, 13–15, 19
Gregory of Nyssa, 3
Grudem, Wayne, 13, 54–55, 129
Guillebaud, Harold, 18n, 129

Hasker, William, 69, 70n, 129
Hay, David, 24, 129,
heaven, x, 1–2, 6, 17, 23–24, 27, 32n, 44n, 45, 48, 54, 67–68, 71–72, 74–76, 79, 87–90, 97, 102, 105–23, 125–28, 130, 132
heavenly grief (problem of), 105–23
Helm, Paul, 95, 129
Hermas of Rome, 3
Hick, John, 66, 89, 127, 129
Hillert, Sven, 30n, 129
Himma, Kenneth, 45n, 129
Hodge, Charles, 26n, 129
Hughes, Philip, 80n, 129
Hunt, David, 69n, 129

Ignatius of Antioch, 3
imago Dei, 49, 51n, 115
immortality, xi, 5–7, 17, 19n, 21–22, 51n, 54, 80–84, 104, 125, 129–30, 132

infinite human guilt thesis, 42, 47, 61–63, 79, 125,
Irenaeus of Lyons, 3, 66, 129

Jewett, Robert, 27n, 129
Jordan, Jeff, 95–96, 129, 132,
justice, xi, 5–6, 15, 30n, 33–46, 51, 53–56, 59–62, 73n, 75–77, 79–80, 82, 85, 95, 105, 107–10, 119, 124–32

Kabay, Paul, 40n, 129
Käsemann, Ernst, 26n, 129
Keener, Craig, 26, 129
Kershnar, Stephen, 37n, 47, 73, 129
Kronen, John, 77n, 100n, 106n, 129
Küng, Hans, 86, 130
Kvanvig, Jonathan, 4, 42n, 48n, 86n, 91n, 92n, 130

Le Guin, Ursula, 72n, 130
Leibniz, Gottfried, 81, 130
Lewis, C. S., 43, 44n, 45, 68, 69n, 94n, 102n, 130
Lewis, David, 35–36, 58n, 99n, 130
libertarianism, 65, 67, 69–73, 76, 79, 83–84, 90–93
Locke, John, 112n, 130
Lotz, David, 32, 130
Lukes, Steven, 93n, 130
Luther, Martin, 3

MacDonald, George, 30n, 38n, 55, 62n, 130
MacDonald, Gregory, 21n, 31n, 26n, 28n, 77n, 90n, 92n, 100n, 112n, 130
Mackie, J. L., 57, 130
Marshall, Christopher D., 42n, 130
Marshall, I. Howard, 13, 24, 42n, 130
Martyr, Justin, 3
McKnight, Scot, 24, 130
McLeod-Harrison, Mark, 50n, 51n, 82–85, 104, 130
Melito of Sardis, 3
middle knowledge (divine). *See* molinism.
Miller, Stephen, 10n, 130
Molina, Luis de, 71, 130

Index

Molinism, Molinist, 71–72, 73n, 74, 76, 79
Moo, Douglas, 24n, 130
Morris, Leon, 27n, 130
Mortimore, Geoffrey, 93n, 130
Murray, Michael, 44–45, 88–92, 104, 130

Novatian of Rome, 3

O'Brien, Peter, 28, 130
Oden, Thomas, 4, 34, 130
omnipotence (divine), 9, 57, 68, 71, 86, 130
open theism, 70–71, 74, 79, 84, 129, 132
Origen of Alexandria, 3
original sin, 25–26, 37–38

Packer, J. I., 98–99, 130
Pamphilus of Caesarea, 3
Parry, Robin, 21n, 25–26, 28n, 30, 31n, 77, 90, 92n, 100n, 112n, 131
Patria, Melia, 112n, 132
Paul, the Apostle, ix, 12, 17, 19, 21–31, 59, 68, 128–29, 132,
Peterson, Robert, 8, 9n, 23, 130
Pinnock, Clark, 6, 7n, 20n, 61, 81n, 131
Plantinga, Alvin, 65, 72n, 131
Plato, 80, 81n, 82, 131
Plotinus, 81
Plug Allen, 101–3, 128
Polycarp of Smyrna, 3
Polycrates of Ephesus, 3
power of contrary choice, 65, 67, 72, 74, 90–91
proportionality criterion, 35, 38, 42–43, 46, 53, 55, 75, 124

Reichenbach, Bruce, 64n, 131
Reitan, Eric, 77n, 86, 92–93, 100n, 106n, 111n, 121–22, 129, 131,
restoration, 2, 5, 18, 35, 53, 60–61, 70, 77, 87, 100, 120
retribution, 4n, 12, 36, 40n, 48n, 128
Richards, Jay, 98–99, 131

salvation, 4, 6, 16, 21–30, 59–60, 71–74, 77–80, 85–95, 98–104, 113, 117, 119–21, 124–25, 128–31

Sanders, John, 70, 131
Satan (devil), 11, 13, 18, 31, 37, 64, 94
Saville, Andy, 50–52, 131
Schleiermacher, Friedrich, 106, 110, 121–22, 131
Schreiner, Thomas, 27n, 131
Seymour, Charles, 43, 44n, 45, 131
Shakespeare, William, 35
Shedd, W. G. T., 23n, 131
Socrates, 80–82, 104
Sodom, 13–15, 19
soul-making theodicy, 5, 64–67, 75–79, 89, 125, 131
Spiegel, James, 51n, 66n, 70n, 131,
Stackhouse Jr., John, 7, 10, 17, 131
status principle/argument, 39–42, 45, 47, 61, 129
Stott, John, 20, 27n, 29, 131
Stump, Eleonore, 4, 44n, 49, 53, 127, 132
Swinburne, Richard, 45–46, 64, 115, 132

Talbott, Thomas, 26, 28, 31, 40n, 72n, 73–74, 84, 86, 93–94, 96, 106n, 109–11, 112n, 113n, 114, 121, 128, 132
Tatian of Assyria, 3
Tertullian of Carthage, 3
theodicy. *See* free will defense and soul-making theodicy.
Theophilus of Antioch, 3
torment. *See* eternal conscious torment.
transworld damnation, 72–76

VanArragon, Raymond, 74, 132
virtue, 1, 37–38, 41–42, 66–68, 77, 90–91, 96–97, 111, 114

Walls, Jerry, 4n, 101–3, 117–19, 128, 132
Ware, Bruce, 70n, 132
Weinandy, Thomas, 118n, 132
Wenham, John, 19n, 132
Wesley, John, 69, 101, 132
Woodruff, Bob, 112n, 132
wrath (divine), 11, 14, 18–19, 48, 59–61

www.ingramcontent.com/pod-product-compliance
Lightning Source LLC
Chambersburg PA
CBHW031502160426
43195CB00010BB/1081